THE QuestKids®

in easy steps
BOOKS FOR KIDS

Coding with Scratch

Create Awesome Platform Games

Max Wainewright

To create the games in this book, you will need:

- a computer or laptop with a proper keyboard; an iPad or any other tablet will not work so well.

- an internet connection to connect to the Scratch website.

It is recommended that children should be supervised when using the internet, especially when using a new website. The publishers and the author cannot be held responsible for the content of the websites referred to in this book.

What is Scratch?

Scratch is a computer programming language that is the easiest language for learning coding, and yet it can be used to create impressive computer games and animations. It is ideal for kids to learn coding and is widely used in schools worldwide.

Scratch is a project of the Scratch Foundation, in collaboration with the Lifelong Kindergarten Group at the MIT Media Lab. It is available to download for free at https://scratch.mit.edu

For further help and resources with this book, visit www.maxw.com or thequestkids.com

The QuestKids® series is an imprint of In Easy Steps Limited
16 Hamilton Terrace, Holly Walk, Leamington Spa,
Warwickshire, United Kingdom CV32 4LY
www.ineasysteps.com
www.thequestkids.com

Trademarks
All trademarks are acknowledged as belonging to their respective companies.

ISBN: 978-1-84078-954-6

MIX
Paper from
responsible sources
FSC® C020837

Printed and bound in the United Kingdom

Notice of Liability
Every effort has been made to ensure that this book contains accurate and current information. However, In Easy Steps Limited and the authors shall not be liable for any loss or damage suffered by readers as a result of any information contained herein.

Contributors:
Author: Max Wainewright
Creative Designer: Jo Cowan
Cover & character illustrations:
Marcelo (The Bright Agency)

Acknowledgements
The publisher would like to thank the following sources for the use of their background illustrations:

Dreamstime, iStock, Shutterstock.com

Contents

Coding with Scratch

In this book you will learn how to code your own platform games. If you haven't done much coding before, don't worry – we will cover all the coding concepts you need as we work through the book. Let's start by learning a bit more about how Scratch works.

THE SCRATCH SCREEN

Use the **File** menu to save your work.

Switch between editing **Costumes** and adding **Code** or **Sounds** to your sprite.

Click the **green flag** to run your code.

Objects that move around in Scratch are called **Sprites**.

Join Scratch for free or log in to your account.

Your game will run in the area called the **stage**.

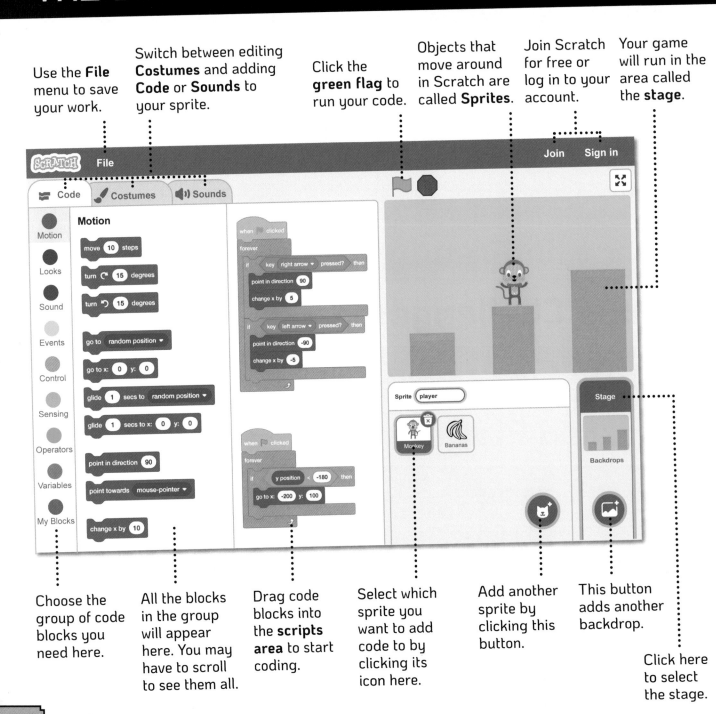

Choose the group of code blocks you need here.

All the blocks in the group will appear here. You may have to scroll to see them all.

Drag code blocks into the **scripts area** to start coding.

Select which sprite you want to add code to by clicking its icon here.

Add another sprite by clicking this button.

This button adds another backdrop.

Click here to select the stage.

4

The book will start by teaching you how to code some simple games.

As you progress through the book the games will get more complex!

You will learn how to add new levels to your games...

...and how to simulate gravity!

Finding blocks

The colour of the block will tell you which group to look through.

*This block is purple, so you'll find it in the **Looks** group.*

Not all blocks will look exactly the way you need them at first.

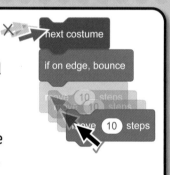

*This block isn't in the **Sensing** group...*

...so find the block that starts with the same command...

...and use the drop-down menu.

You will discover how to make sprites jump from platform to platform.

Joining blocks

Each block in Scratch makes a sprite do something different. To join them together just drag one block so that it snaps onto another.

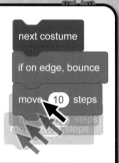

If you want to break blocks apart, you can't pull the top block up.

You need to drag a block away from the bottom of the stack.

Arranging your code

Most of the games in this block use quite a lot of code. To make the code clearer it is divided up into different sections or **scripts**.

You'll learn how to create your own code blocks to reuse in your own games.

Ouch!

*Don't try to join the top of curved **event** blocks to other blocks.*

The curved event block is the start of a separate script.

When you have a lot of code, use these controls to zoom in or zoom out of your code.

This button puts your code back to normal size.

Saving your work

You can save your game by downloading a copy of it to your computer.

Click **File** > **Save to your computer**.

Saved work is usually found in your Downloads folder.

Click **Load from your computer**, then browse to your file to get it back.

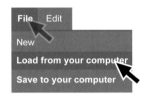

Click **File** > **Load from your computer**.

SAVING ONLINE

It is a little easier to save your work if you have a Scratch account. Your work then gets saved online. This means you can carry on with your work on a different computer. It also allows you to share your completed game. Other people will be allowed to comment on your games too. **Check with an adult before signing up to get a Scratch account.**

 Click **Join Scratch** and follow the instructions to create an account.

 To log in to your account, click **Sign in**. You'll need your username and password.

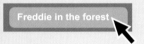 Type a name for your game in the box at the top.

 Click **File** > **Save now** to save your work online.

 Click the folder icon to see all the files that you have saved (called **My Stuff**).

 To load a game to play it or carry on coding, click **See inside**.

It's a good idea to save your work after every step.

Testing your code

 After each coding step in this book you will usually see a green flag.

This is reminding you to run your code and check it works. If it doesn't work, check back through the code you have just added. Make sure:

- You used the correct blocks (some look very similar!).
- You have typed in the correct numbers.
- You have used minus and plus numbers correctly.
- Loops and if then blocks are in the correct place.

Sometimes it's a good idea to delete some of your code and start over again.

Later on in this book you'll learn how to add background music to a game.

And how to use variables to keep score and track how fast things move!

Setting colours

The colour slider lets you pick just over a million different shades.

To help you find the right shade you will find colour helpers like this one.

Set each of the sliders to the numbers shown here.

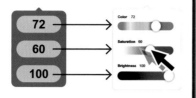

Once you have used a colour, the Pipette tool can be used to "pick up" the exact shade.

I'll show you how to use the Pipette in your code on Page 19.

Drawing backgrounds

Scratch has lots of great ready-made background pictures, called backdrops. But for most of the games in this book you'll be creating your own backdrops. That way, you'll be able to design all sorts of different levels for your platform games. Here are some of the tools you will be using:

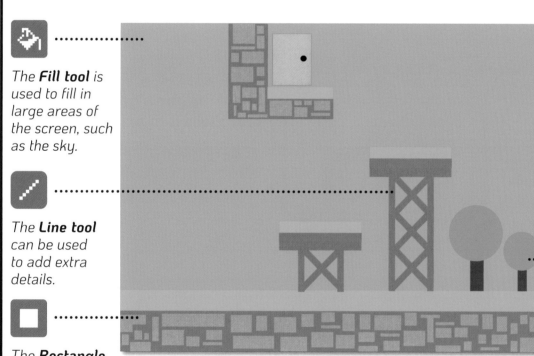

*The **Fill tool** is used to fill in large areas of the screen, such as the sky.*

*The **Line tool** can be used to add extra details.*

*The **Rectangle tool** is used to draw platforms and sections of the ground.*

*The **Colour tool** is very important. Different colours will tell the sprites whether they are in mid-air or standing on the ground!*

*The **Circle tool** can be used to draw ovals or circles.*

If things go wrong with your backdrop use the Undo or Redo button.

Undo   Redo

Normal size

Zoom out   Zoom in

Zoom in to add detail to your picture.

Banana Bonanza

In this simple game you will learn the basics of how to move a character sprite around the screen. Pressing the left and right arrow keys will make the cat move. Simple animation will make it look as though it is walking. More code will make the bananas the cat eats disappear.

1 Start Scratch

Go to the Scratch website.

scratch.mit.edu

2 Start creating

At the top of the page click **Create**.

3 Make space

There may be a green help video box. **Close** it to make more space.

4 Move right

We need the cat to move around when the arrow keys are pressed. Drag in the following code blocks:

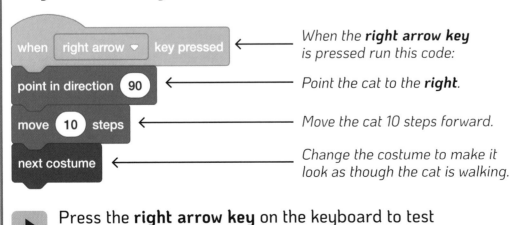

when **right arrow** key pressed ← *When the **right arrow key** is pressed run this code:*

point in direction 90 ← *Point the cat to the **right**.*

move 10 steps ← *Move the cat 10 steps forward.*

next costume ← *Change the costume to make it look as though the cat is walking.*

→ Press the **right arrow key** on the keyboard to test your code. The cat should slowly walk to the right!

Turn back to pages 4–5 for help finding the code blocks you need.

5 Move left

Drag in these blocks to make the cat move left when the left arrow is pressed:

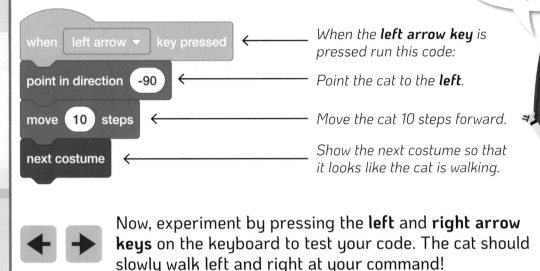

*When the **left arrow key** is pressed run this code:*

*Point the cat to the **left**.*

Move the cat 10 steps forward.

Show the next costume so that it looks like the cat is walking.

Now, experiment by pressing the **left** and **right arrow keys** on the keyboard to test your code. The cat should slowly walk left and right at your command!

Distances in Scratch are measured in Steps. A Step is the same size as a Pixel. Pixels are the tiny dots on the screen that make up a picture.

I turn upside down when I move left!

Help me!

6 Rotation style

To keep the sprite the correct way up we will set its rotation style.

*When the **green flag** is clicked, run this code:*

Stop the cat rotating — just make it face left or right.

Click the **green flag** to test your code. Try using the arrow keys to move left and right. The cat will still walk each way, but now it should stay the right way up.

HOW DOES ANIMATION WORK IN SCRATCH?

next costume

Just as we can wear more than one set of clothes, sprites in Scratch can have more than one **costume**.

By switching from one costume to another we get a simple animation effect. Each costume must be drawn carefully for this to work.

We'll learn more about costumes later

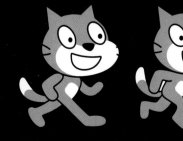

Costume1   *Costume2*

7 Cat food

We need to give the cat something to eat.

Click the **Choose a Sprite** button (in the bottom-right corner of the screen).

8 Take your pick

Choose something for the cat to eat and click it.

9 Position the banana

Drag the banana downwards so that it is lined up with the cat.

USING SENSING BLOCKS

It can be tricky fitting the light blue sensing blocks into orange control blocks.

*Start with a **wait until** block from the **Control** group.*

*Drag a **touching mouse-pointer** block inside the **wait until** block.*

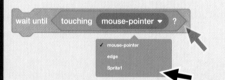

*Click the **mouse-pointer** drop-down and then select **Sprite1**.*

Now, your blocks are ready.

10 Code the banana

So the cat can eat the bananas, we need to add some code.

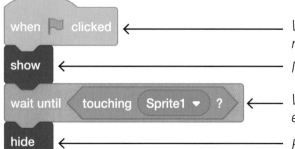

When the **green flag** is clicked, run the code below:

Make sure the banana is visible.

Wait until Sprite1 (the cat) is close enough to touch the banana.

Hide the banana.

Click the **green flag** to test your code. Use the arrow keys to move the cat towards the banana. It should disappear when the cat touches it.

Mmm... bananas!

11 Add a background

Finally, we need to add a background picture for our game.

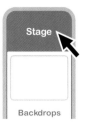 **Click the Stage icon** (on the right-hand side of the screen).

 Click the **Backdrops** tab (at the top left of the screen).

 Click on **Convert to Bitmap**. This will give us simpler tools to use.

If you make a mistake when drawing, click the Undo button.

12 Start drawing

Now, draw the sky and some grass — in later games we'll have multiple levels, but keep this one simple.

 Click the **Fill** tool.

Mix a blue colour.

| 56 |
| 87 |
| 91 |

 Fill the sky in blue.

 Pick the **Rectangle** tool.

Make a green colour.

| 34 |
| 60 |
| 78 |

 Drag out a rectangle to be the grass.

 Position the cat on the grass. Try out your game by clicking the **green flag**. Use the arrow keys to move the cat left or right and eat the banana.

Use these numbers to help mix the colours you need.

Challenges

- Add some different sorts of food for the cat to eat. (Follow steps 5-8 if you are stuck.)

- Create extra food by duplicating the banana. (Click the right mouse button on the banana sprite icon and choose one of the options.)

- Try remaking the game with a different animal instead of the cat.

Jumposaurus

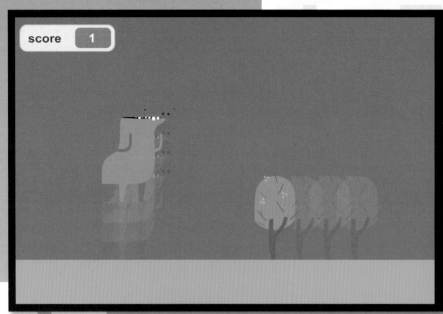

score | 1

Although this is not really a platform game we will use it to start learning ways to make sprites jump. The dinosaur will have to jump over trees as they scroll across the screen. If it lands on one it will be game over! A score variable will keep track of the number of trees jumped!

1 Start Scratch

Go to the Scratch website and click **Create** to start a new file.

scratch.mit.edu

2 No cats

We won't need a cat. Click on the bin to delete it.

Sprite1

3 Prepare the background

Select the stage so that we can draw a background.

Click the **Stage** icon.

Click the **Backdrops** tab.

Click the **Convert to Bitmap** button.

4 Start drawing

Draw the sky and some grass, the way we did in the previous game.

Pick the **Fill** tool.

Make a blue colour.

56
87
91

Fill the sky in blue.

Click the **Rectangle** tool.

Mix a green colour.

34
60
78

Drag out a rectangle to be the grass.

5 New sprite

We need a replacement for the cat, so click **Choose a Sprite**.

6 Find a dinosaur

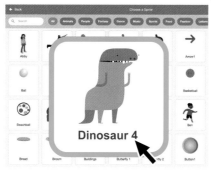

Scroll through the sprites and click on **Dinosaur 4**.

X AND Y COORDINATES

Sprites are positioned on the stage by using X and Y values, or coordinates.

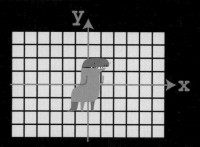

We can move a sprite left or right by changing its **x value**. Changing its **y value** will make it move up or down. We will learn more about coordinates later in the book.

7 Jump!

How well can dinosaurs jump? It's time to find out! Drag in the code below:

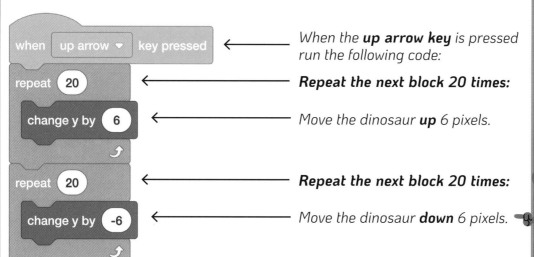

```
when  up arrow ▼  key pressed
repeat  20
    change y by  6
repeat  20
    change y by  -6
```

When the **up arrow key** is pressed run the following code:

Repeat the next block 20 times:

*Move the dinosaur **up** 6 pixels.*

Repeat the next block 20 times:

*Move the dinosaur **down** 6 pixels.*

> Using a minus number makes the dinosaur move down.

Press the **up arrow key** on the keyboard to test your code. See how well your dinosaur can jump!

8 New sprite

The dinosaur will need something to jump over.

Click the **Choose a Sprite** button.

9 Pick a tree

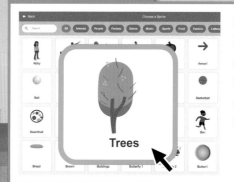

Scroll through the sprites to find the sprite called **Trees**. Click it.

10 Keeping score

We want the game to keep track of how many trees the dinosaur has jumped over. To do this we will make a special counter called a variable.

Choose the **Variables** group.

Click **Make a Variable**.

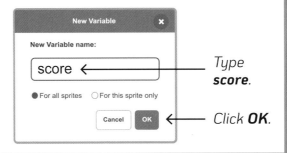

*Type **score**.*

*Click **OK**.*

> Make sure you change the drop-down menu from **my variable** to **score**.

11 Code the tree

Get the tree scrolling across the screen by dragging in this code:

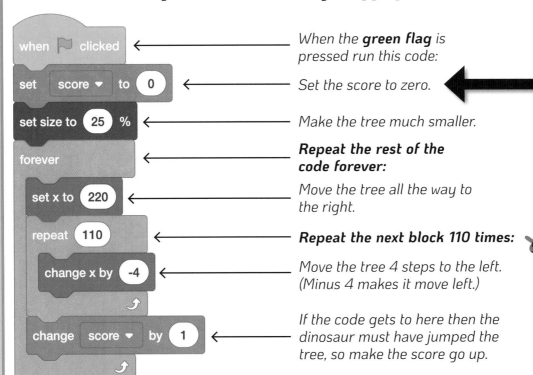

*When the **green flag** is pressed run this code:*

Set the score to zero.

Make the tree much smaller.

Repeat the rest of the code forever:

Move the tree all the way to the right.

Repeat the next block 110 times:

Move the tree 4 steps to the left. (Minus 4 makes it move left.)

If the code gets to here then the dinosaur must have jumped the tree, so make the score go up.

Click the **green flag** to test your code. The tree should slowly travel across the screen.

> This loop will slowly change the x value from 220 to minus 220, making the tree slowly move all the way across the stage.

12 Select the dinosaur

We need to add more code to the dinosaur, so click on it to select it.

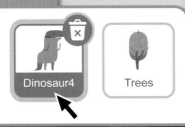

13 Code for the dinosaur

This code will shrink the dinosaur, animate it and check to see where it lands.

Click the Costumes tab if you want to see how the animation works.

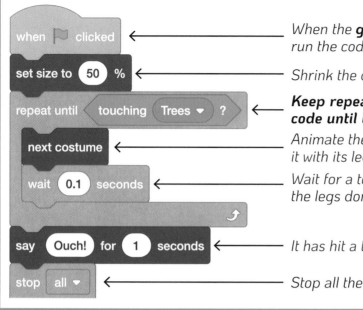

*When the **green flag** is pressed run the code below:*

Shrink the dinosaur to half its size.

Keep repeating the next blocks of code until the dinosaur hits a tree.

Animate the dinosaur by showing it with its legs in a different place.

Wait for a tenth of a second so that the legs don't move too quickly.

It has hit a tree, so show a message.

Stop all the code (including the tree).

14 Final touches

Get everything ready to play your game!

Click the **green flag** to run the code and shrink the dinosaur.

Now, click the **Stop** button.

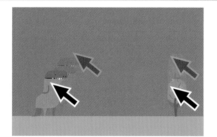

Position both the sprites so they are touching the ground, like this.

Now, test your code by playing the game! If the dinosaur hits the tree, the game should end. What is your best score?

Boing!

Challenges

- Experiment with the repeat 20 loops. What happens if you use bigger numbers?
- Try to make the tree move more quickly. You may need to change the repeat 110 loop too.
- Change the size of the tree. How does this affect the game?
- Make the tree grow slowly during the game. Try adding a **change size** block after the **change score** block.

Space Dog

Our first proper platform game will be set in space, on the planet Blokk. Our space dog, Dot, will travel across the surface of the planet. Pressing arrow keys will make Dot move left, right or jump upwards. We will use code to check if Dot has hit the red ground of the planet or is standing on the purple grass.

Here is our plan for the game. Coders sometimes call a plan for how something works an "algorithm".

HOW THE GAME WORKS

The up arrow key will run a loop. The loop will change the y value of the dog, making it move up.

The dog will only be allowed to start jumping if it is touching the purple grass.

If the dog is in the air it must fall down slowly. Changing its y value will do this.

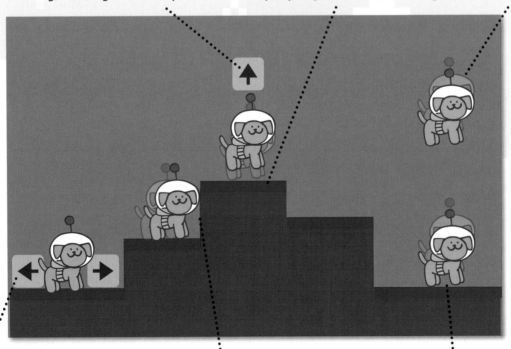

The left and right arrow keys will change the dog's x value, making it move left or right.

If the dog hits something red it must stop. An **if block** will check for this and move it back 10 steps.

When the dog touches the grass it needs to stop falling. This is done by making it move up very slightly, giving a bouncing effect.

website and create a new file.

scratch.mit.edu

It's dogs not cats in this game. Click on the bin to delete the cat.

Sprite1

New background

Click the **Choose a Backdrop** button (it's in the bottom-right corner of the screen).

4 Choose stars

Stars

Scroll through the backgrounds to find the one called **Stars**. Click it.

5 Select the correct tab

Backdrops

Click the **Backdrops** tab so that we can draw on top of the Stars background.

Use these numbers to help mix the dark red colour.

0
100
81

6 Draw the ground

We will start by drawing the planet in red. Remember, the colour will tell our code when it needs to make things happen, so stick to one shade of red for now.

 Select the **Rectangle** tool.

Mix a dark red colour.

Click the Undo button if things go wrong with your rectangles.

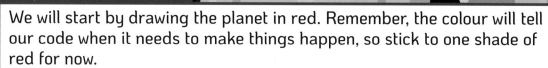

Draw a series of rectangles to build up a sort of staircase platform across the planet.

Now, draw some thin grass on top of the ground. The grass on planet Blokk is purple.

Choose purple.

83
91
72

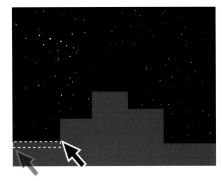

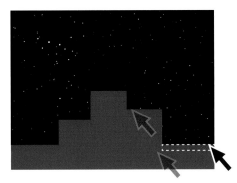

Add purple grass **on the top** of each red platform. For the game to work properly, it's important you stick to these colours for now, and put grass on each platform.

8 Add a sprite

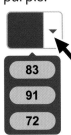

Click the **Choose a Sprite** button.

9 Space dog

Scroll through to find the dog called **Dot**. Click on it.

Woof! Woof!

DRAWING TIPS

Once you have drawn a shape in Scratch, you can still make changes to it.

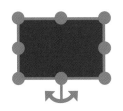

Use the handles to resize or rotate the shape.

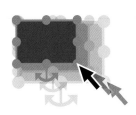

Drag the middle of the shape to move it.

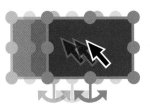

You can also use the arrow keys to nudge it.

To fix the shape place, click any outside the shap

Use the U button if y to try aga

This code will make the dog move left or right when the arrow keys are pressed. Click the **Code** tab then drag the code in.

will respond more smoothly if the keys are held down.

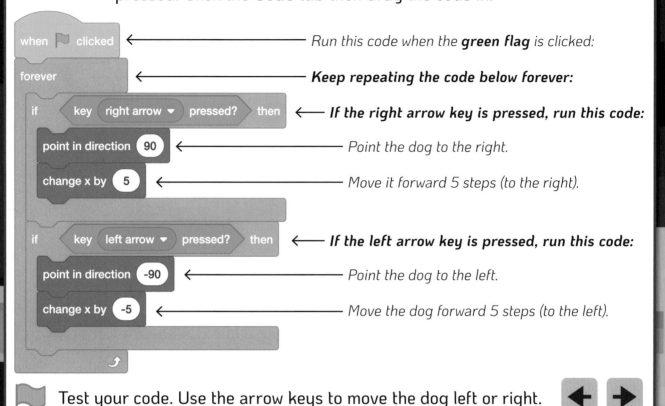

when ⚑ clicked ← Run this code when the **green flag** is clicked:

forever ← **Keep repeating the code below forever:**

if ⟨ key right arrow ▾ pressed? ⟩ then ← **If the right arrow key is pressed, run this code:**

point in direction 90 ← Point the dog to the right.

change x by 5 ← Move it forward 5 steps (to the right).

if ⟨ key left arrow ▾ pressed? ⟩ then ← **If the left arrow key is pressed, run this code:**

point in direction -90 ← Point the dog to the left.

change x by -5 ← Move the dog forward 5 steps (to the left).

⚑ Test your code. Use the arrow keys to move the dog left or right.

11 Set up and check for collisions

Now, add some more code to get the dog ready and to check if it has bumped into a red wall.

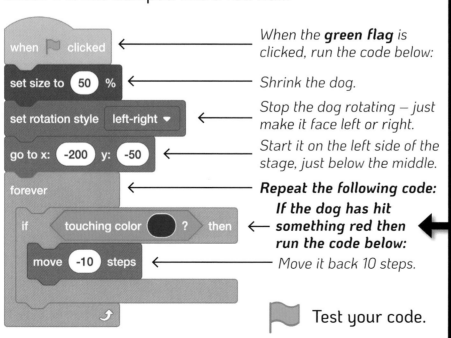

when ⚑ clicked ← When the **green flag** is clicked, run the code below:

set size to 50 % ← Shrink the dog.

set rotation style left-right ▾ ← Stop the dog rotating — just make it face left or right.

go to x: -200 y: -50 ← Start it on the left side of the stage, just below the middle.

forever ← **Repeat the following code:**

if ⟨ touching color ⬤ ? ⟩ then ← **If the dog has hit something red then run the code below:**

move -10 steps ← Move it back 10 steps.

⚑ Test your code.

SENSING COLOURS

We need to set the exact shade of red for the code to work here.

 Start with an **if then** block from the **Control** group.

 Drop a **touching color** block inside it.

 Click the current colour to open the menu.

 Click the Pipette.

 Move the mouse over the stage and click the colour you want.

 The block is ready to use.

Although we aren't going to simulate gravity, we need to make the dog move down if it is in the air. If it hits the purple grass then it needs to stop falling. Add this code:

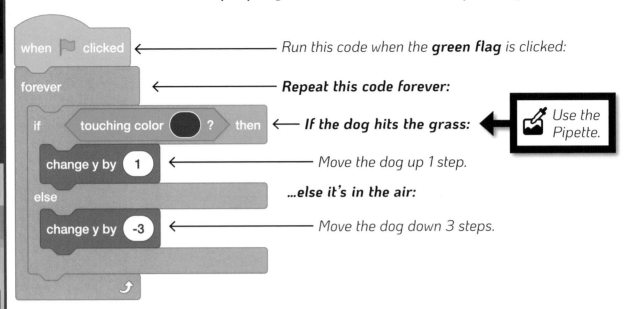

when ⚑ clicked ← — *Run this code when the **green flag** is clicked:*

forever ← — **Repeat this code forever:**

if ⟨ touching color ● ? ⟩ then ← — **If the dog hits the grass:** ← *Use the Pipette.*

change y by 1 ← — *Move the dog up 1 step.*

else — **...else it's in the air:**

change y by -3 ← — *Move the dog down 3 steps.*

⚑ Test your code. Check the dog stops falling down when it hits the grass.

13 Jump!

Finally, we need to add code to make the dog jump up when the **space** key is pressed.

Before we let the dog jump up, we need to check it is on the grass.

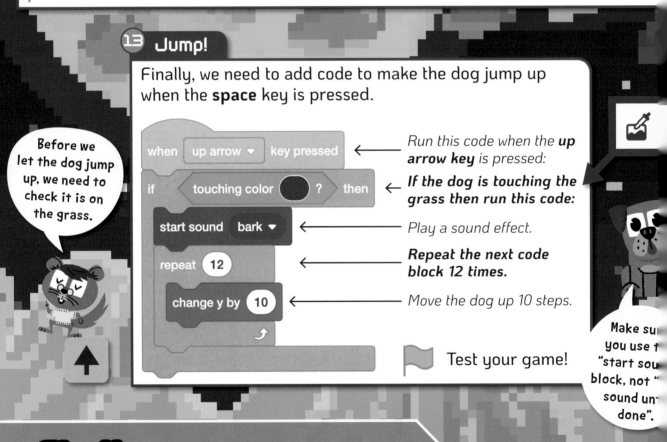

when up arrow ▼ key pressed ← — *Run this code when the **up arrow key** is pressed:*

if ⟨ touching color ● ? ⟩ then ← — **If the dog is touching the grass then run this code:**

start sound bark ▼ ← — *Play a sound effect.*

repeat 12 ← — **Repeat the next code block 12 times.**

change y by 10 ← — *Move the dog up 10 steps.*

⚑ Test your game!

Make su you use t "start sou block, not " sound un done".

Challenges

- Add some more platforms to the backdrop. Remember to use the correct colours.
- Try to make the dog jump up more quickly.
- Add some food for the dog to eat. Look at the code in the first game to help you.

Polar Penguin

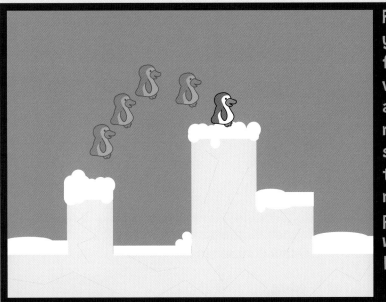

Polar Penguin will develop your platform coding skills further. We will use a variable to store the speed at which the penguin is moving up or down. This will simulate gravity and make the game more fun and more realistic! As with previous games, key presses will make the penguin move left or right.

HOW THE GAME WORKS

A variable called ySpeed will store how fast the penguin is going up or down.

When the up arrow key is pressed, the ySpeed variable will get set to 10. This will make it move up quickly.

All the time the penguin is in the air, the code will keep changing the ySpeed variable by -0.5...

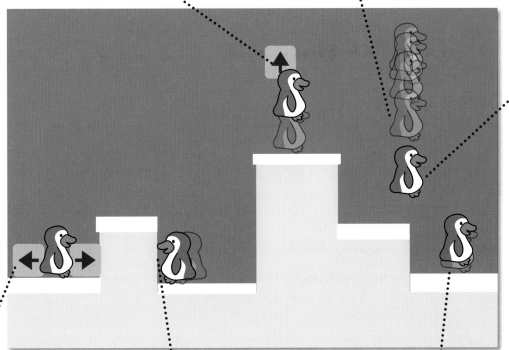

...this will make it fall more quickly, accelerating back to the earth.

The left and right arrow keys will change the penguin's x value, making it move left or right.

When the penguin hits some pale blue ice it must stop. An if block will check for this and move it back 10 steps.

When it touches the snow it needs to stop falling. This is done by setting its ySpeed variable to 1, making it move up again very slowly.

1 Start Scratch

Go to the Scratch website and create a new file.

scratch.mit.edu

2 Delete the cat

We don't need the cat so click on the bin to delete it.

Sprite1

Brrr!

3 Prepare the background

Get ready to draw the background for our game.

Click the **Backdrops** tab.

Click the **Convert to Bitmap** button.

4 Draw the sky

Draw a blue sky.

Pick the **Fill** tool.

Mix blue.

| 56 |
| 87 |
| 91 |

Fill the sky in blue.

5 Draw the ice

Begin by drawing the ice in pale blue. Don't forget the colour will tell our code when it needs to make things happen, so stick to one shade of pale blue.

| 54 |
| 24 |
| 100 |

 Select the **Rectangle** tool.

 Make a pale blue colour.

If things go wrong with your drawing, click the Undo button.

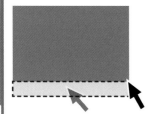  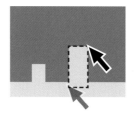 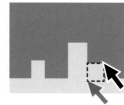

Use the Rectangle tool to draw some different-sized platforms across the ice.

6 Add some snow

We need a different colour on top of each platform, so draw a thin layer of snow.

Choose white.

| 0 |
| 0 |
| 100 |

Remember, for the game to work properly it's important you use these colours.

7 More snow!

 Use the Brush tool to add some extra snow!

8 Cracks in the ice

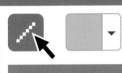 Now, use the Line tool to make cracks in the ice.

| 56 |
| 33 |
| 91 |

9 Add a sprite

Next, we need to add the main player sprite.

 Click the **Choose a Sprite** button.

10 Pick a penguin

Penguin 2

Scroll through the sprites and click on **Penguin 2**.

Woof!

11 Add a variable

So that we can make the penguin fall faster and jump more realistically, we are going to need a variable to store its vertical speed. This will store how much the penguin needs to move up or down — how much its y value changes.

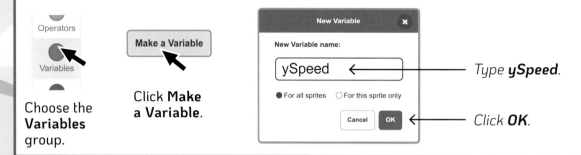

Choose the **Variables** group.

Click **Make a Variable**.

Type **ySpeed**.

Click **OK**.

12 Left and right

Add code to make the penguin move left or right when the arrow keys are pressed.

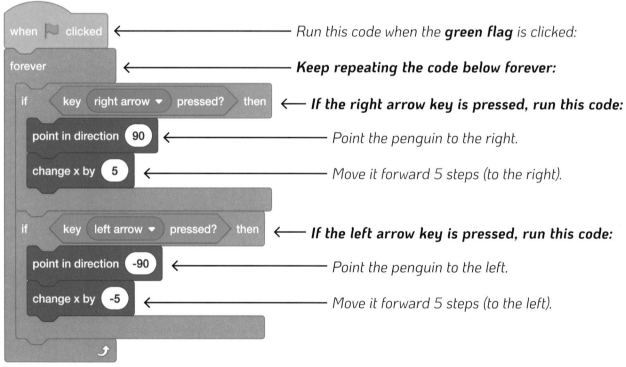

Run this code when the **green flag** is clicked:

Keep repeating the code below forever:

← **If the right arrow key is pressed, run this code:**

Point the penguin to the right.

Move it forward 5 steps (to the right).

← **If the left arrow key is pressed, run this code:**

Point the penguin to the left.

Move it forward 5 steps (to the left).

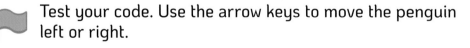 Test your code. Use the arrow keys to move the penguin left or right.

Ouch!

Add this code to get the penguin ready and to check if it has hit some ice.

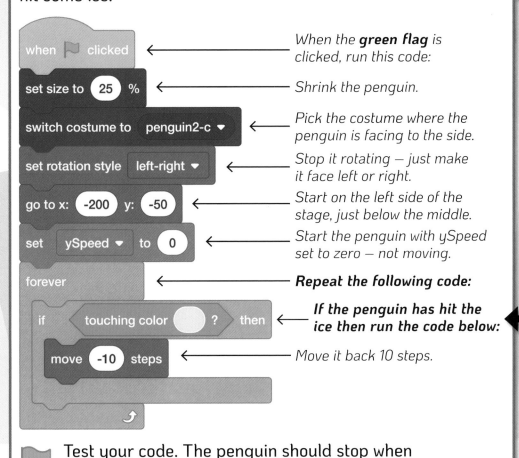

*When the **green flag** is clicked, run this code:*

Shrink the penguin.

Pick the costume where the penguin is facing to the side.

Stop it rotating — just make it face left or right.

Start on the left side of the stage, just below the middle.

Start the penguin with ySpeed set to zero — not moving.

Repeat the following code:

If the penguin has hit the ice then run the code below:

Move it back 10 steps.

Collision detection means checking to see if a sprite has hit something.

 Use the Pipette.

Test your code. The penguin should stop when it hits some ice.

Check carefully whether you need a change variable or set variable block. Don't get them mixed up!!

USING VARIABLE CODE BLOCKS

To **set** the value of a variable we need to use the **set** block:

```
set  ySpeed ▼  to  1
```

This would **set** the ySpeed variable to 1 until anything else changes it.

1 1 1 1 1 1 1

To **change** the value of a variable we use the **change** block:

```
change  ySpeed ▼  by  1
```

This will **change** the ySpeed by 1. This would make ySpeed variable increase, each time the block is used.

1 2 3 4 5 6 7

ySpeed

To **use** the value of a variable we need this block.

```
ySpeed
change y by  10
```

```
change y by  ySpeed
```

Drop the small orange block inside another code block.

This will **change** the y value of a sprite by whatever the value of the variable is.

14 Up and down

Finally, we will add code to make the penguin move up and down.

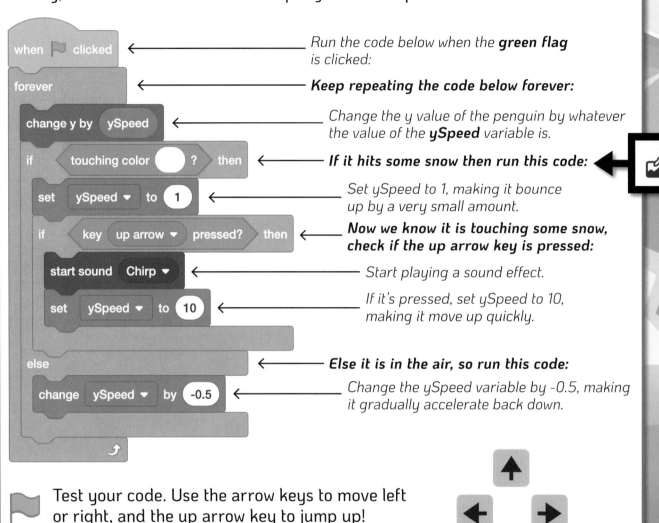

when ⚑ clicked ← *Run the code below when the **green flag** is clicked:*

forever ← ***Keep repeating the code below forever:***

change y by ySpeed ← *Change the y value of the penguin by whatever the value of the **ySpeed** variable is.*

if touching color ⬤ ? then ← ***If it hits some snow then run this code:***

set ySpeed ▾ to 1 ← *Set ySpeed to 1, making it bounce up by a very small amount.*

if key up arrow ▾ pressed? then ← ***Now we know it is touching some snow, check if the up arrow key is pressed:***

start sound Chirp ▾ ← *Start playing a sound effect.*

set ySpeed ▾ to 10 ← *If it's pressed, set ySpeed to 10, making it move up quickly.*

else ← ***Else it is in the air, so run this code:***

change ySpeed ▾ by -0.5 ← *Change the ySpeed variable by -0.5, making it gradually accelerate back down.*

⚑ Test your code. Use the arrow keys to move left or right, and the up arrow key to jump up!

Challenges

- Change the platforms on the backdrop. Make them bigger or smaller. Remember to use the correct colours. Add some more snow to create a slope and see what happens.

- Try to make the penguin jump up more quickly. (Change some code in box 14.)

- Try to increase the effect of gravity so that the penguin falls more quickly (box 14).

- Add something for the penguin to collect or eat. Look at the code in the first game to help you.

Monkey City

Monkey City uses the techniques from the previous games to allow a monkey to make its way across the skyscrapers of a city. The game introduces levels – when one part of the game has been completed, another challenge is shown. This is done by connecting together different backdrops. We will also add code to check if the monkey has fallen down between buildings.

HOW THE GAME WORKS

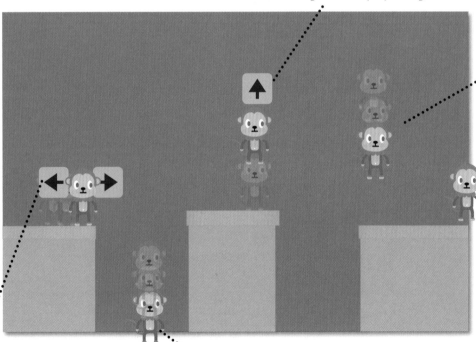

Pressing the up arrow key sets the ySpeed variable to 10. This will make the monkey move up quickly.

When the monkey is in the air, the ySpeed variable will keep changing by -0.5, making it fall back down to the ground.

Each level is completed by getting to the right-hand side. An **if block** checks to see if the monkey's x value is greater than 240. If it is, then the next level will start.

As with previous games, these arrow keys will change the monkey's x value, making it move.

If the monkey falls between the buildings it will fall "out of the game" and have to start the level again. This is done by checking if its y value is less than -240.

level 1

A variable will store the current level.

Each level will be drawn on a separate backdrop.

1 Start Scratch

Go to the Scratch website and create a new file.

scratch.mit.edu

2 Delete the cat

We won't need the cat so click on the bin to delete it.

Sprite1

3 Prepare the background

Get ready to draw the background for our game.

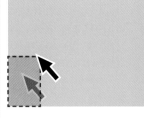

Click the **Backdrops** tab.

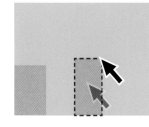

Click **Convert to Bitmap**.

4 Draw the sky

Draw a blue sky.

Pick the **Fill** tool.

Mix a blue colour.

55
54
100

Fill the sky in blue.

5 Draw the skyscrapers

Start drawing the buildings in violet. Don't forget the colour will tell our code when it needs to make things happen, so stick to this colour. You can add more details later.

Select the **Rectangle** tool.

Make a pinkish colour for the skyscrapers.

74
24
100

Draw three different-sized rectangles across the skyline. Leave gaps between them.

Click Undo if things go wrong.

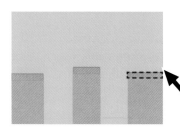

6 Put a roof on top

For the code to work, we need a different colour on top. Draw the roofs in orange.

Choose orange.

9
67
100

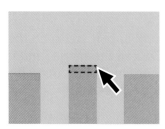

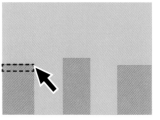

Remember — for the game to work properly, it's important you use these colours.

7 Make another level

Add another backdrop to design the next level of your game.

Hover

Move your mouse to *hover* over the **Choose a Backdrop** button in the bottom-left of the screen.

Don't click it!

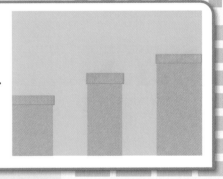

A menu like this will appear.

Move your mouse up to the **Paint** option and click it.

8 Convert to bitmap

Click the **Convert to Bitmap** button.

9 Repeat!

Now, **repeat steps 4, 5 and 6** to design the second level of your game.

Make it a bit trickier than the first one.

10 Repeat!

Create the third level of your game by **repeating steps 4, 5 and 6** again.

This level should be even harder!

Keep the levels fairly simple for now. You can always go back and add some extra details later. You just need a few levels so that you can get all the code working.

11 Check

Before you go on to start coding, check your screen looks roughly like this.

If it doesn't, go back and check you have carried out each step correctly.

12 Add a sprite

Next, we need to add the main player sprite.

Click **Choose a Sprite**.

13 Find a monkey

Monkey

Scroll down through the sprites and click on the **Monkey** sprite.

14 Add the speed variable

We'll use the same technique as in the previous game to store how fast the monkey is moving up or down. Make a variable called ySpeed.

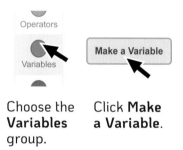

Operators

Variables

Choose the **Variables** group.

Click **Make a Variable**.

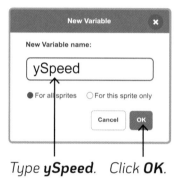

New Variable

New Variable name:

ySpeed

● For all sprites   ○ For this sprite only

Cancel   OK

*Type **ySpeed**.*   *Click **OK**.*

15 Which level?

So that we know which level the game is on, we will make another variable and call it Level. It will start at 1, then go up as each level is completed.

Make a Variable

Click **Make a Variable**.

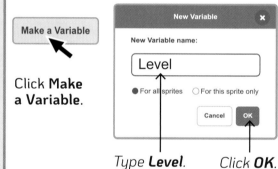

New Variable

New Variable name:

Level

● For all sprites   ○ For this sprite only

Cancel   OK

*Type **Level**.*   *Click **OK**.*

16 Add a sound effect

We will choose an extra sound effect to play when the monkey jumps up.

 Sounds

Select the **Sounds** tab.

Click **Choose a Sound**.

17 Find the sound

Boing

Scroll through the sounds and click on **Boing**.

HIDING OR SHOWING VARIABLES

You can choose which variables are shown in the top left of the stage.

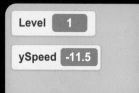

Level   1

ySpeed   -11.5

While you are coding, it's useful to see the value of all variables. Once a game is finished, you don't need players to see them all.

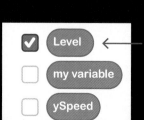

☑ Level
☐ my variable
☐ ySpeed

Just tick the variables you want people to see.

Click the **Code** tab, then start adding some simple code. These blocks will make the monkey move left and right.

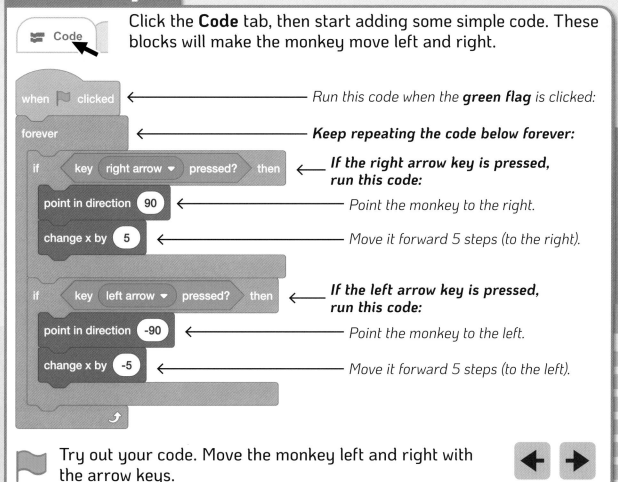

when ▶ clicked ← — Run this code when the **green flag** is clicked:

forever ← — **Keep repeating the code below forever:**

if ⟨ key right arrow ▾ pressed? ⟩ then ← — **If the right arrow key is pressed, run this code:**

point in direction 90 ← — Point the monkey to the right.

change x by 5 ← — Move it forward 5 steps (to the right).

if ⟨ key left arrow ▾ pressed? ⟩ then ← — **If the left arrow key is pressed, run this code:**

point in direction -90 ← — Point the monkey to the left.

change x by -5 ← — Move it forward 5 steps (to the left).

🏳 Try out your code. Move the monkey left and right with the arrow keys.

◀ ▶

To check the levels are working properly, add this bit of code in next. It will see if the monkey has got to the right-hand side of the screen by checking its x value. If the x value is bigger than 240, the money has got there.

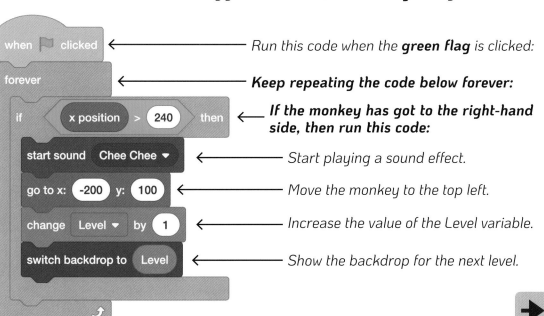

when ▶ clicked ← — Run this code when the **green flag** is clicked:

forever ← — **Keep repeating the code below forever:**

if ⟨ x position > 240 ⟩ then ← — **If the monkey has got to the right-hand side, then run this code:**

start sound Chee Chee ▾ ← — Start playing a sound effect.

go to x: -200 y: 100 ← — Move the monkey to the top left.

change Level ▾ by 1 ← — Increase the value of the Level variable.

switch backdrop to Level ← — Show the backdrop for the next level.

The platforms won't work yet, but you should see each level show up.

🏳 Test your code. When the monkey gets to the right-hand side, the next level should appear and the monkey will move back to the left.

20 Setup and collision detection

Add this code to get the monkey ready and to check if it has hit something.

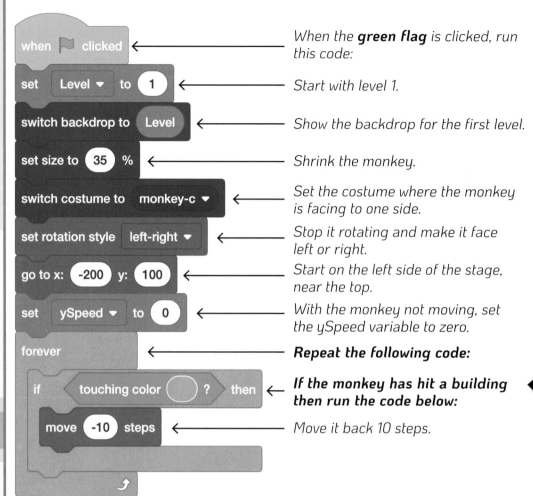

when [flag] clicked ← When the **green flag** is clicked, run *this code:*

set Level ▾ to 1 ← Start with level 1.

switch backdrop to Level ← Show the backdrop for the first level.

set size to 35 % ← Shrink the monkey.

switch costume to monkey-c ▾ ← Set the costume where the monkey *is facing to one side.*

set rotation style left-right ▾ ← Stop it rotating and make it face *left or right.*

go to x: -200 y: 100 ← Start on the left side of the stage, *near the top.*

set ySpeed ▾ to 0 ← With the monkey not moving, set *the ySpeed variable to zero.*

forever ← **Repeat the following code:**

if touching color ( ) ? then ← **If the monkey has hit a building then run the code below:**

move -10 steps ← Move it back 10 steps.

Use the Pipette.

[flag] Test your code. Check the monkey stops when it hits a building.

21 The end of the world!

In most platform games it is possible to fall through the bottom of the screen. This sometimes loses a life. We will add code so that if the monkey falls down a gap it will start the level again. Checking the y value will allow us to do this.

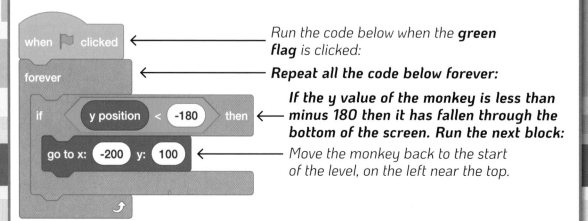

when [flag] clicked ← Run the code below when the **green flag** is clicked:

forever ← **Repeat all the code below forever:**

if y position < -180 then ← **If the y value of the monkey is less than minus 180 then it has fallen through the bottom of the screen. Run the next block:**

go to x: -200 y: 100 ← Move the monkey back to the start *of the level, on the left near the top.*

We need to put an if block inside an if else block. This is called "nesting". It can be fiddly to place blocks like this, so do it first.

This code will allow the monkey to move up and down.

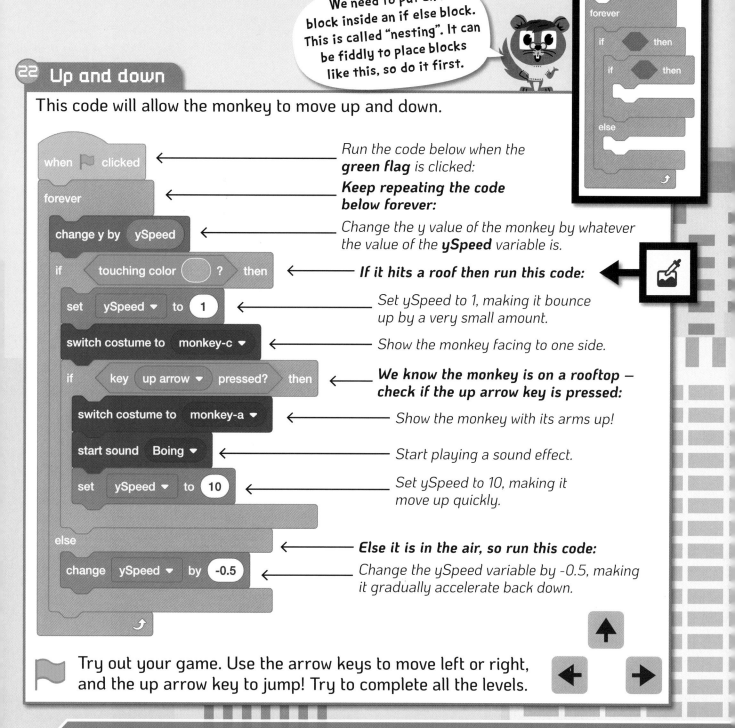

when 🏳 **clicked** ← Run the code below when the **green flag** is clicked:

forever ← **Keep repeating the code below forever:**

change y by ySpeed ← Change the y value of the monkey by whatever the value of the **ySpeed** variable is.

if touching color ⬤ **?** **then** ← **If it hits a roof then run this code:**

set ySpeed **to** 1 ← Set ySpeed to 1, making it bounce up by a very small amount.

switch costume to monkey-c ← Show the monkey facing to one side.

if key up arrow pressed? **then** ← **We know the monkey is on a rooftop — check if the up arrow key is pressed:**

switch costume to monkey-a ← Show the monkey with its arms up!

start sound Boing ← Start playing a sound effect.

set ySpeed **to** 10 ← Set ySpeed to 10, making it move up quickly.

else ← **Else it is in the air, so run this code:** Change the ySpeed variable by -0.5, making it gradually accelerate back down.

change ySpeed **by** -0.5 ←

🏳 Try out your game. Use the arrow keys to move left or right, and the up arrow key to jump! Try to complete all the levels.

Challenges

- Add more levels. Look back to Step 9 for a reminder.
- Experiment with the speed the monkey falls down at and how quickly it jumps up.
- Draw some windows on the skyscrapers and clouds on the backdrop.
- Add some bananas for the monkey to eat. Use the code from the first game to help you.
- Change what happens when the monkey falls down through the bottom of the screen. Make another variable called "lives", and make the lives go down (change by -1) when the monkey falls out of the screen. Use an if block to make the game stop when there are no lives left.

Haunted House

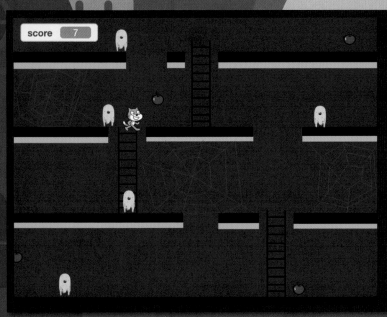

score 7

Haunted House uses many of the coding techniques we've learnt so far, but it is a different kind of platform game. Multiple floor levels are shown on the screen at the same time. Magic ladders will make the player move up automatically. Blue ghosts will float around on each floor. The player has to avoid the ghosts and collect or eat as many apples as possible. Creepy music will make it a very spooky experience!

HOW THE GAME WORKS

The score variable will count how many apples the cat has eaten.

♪ Creepy music will play in the background.

The ySpeed variable will control how fast the cat moves up or down — the same way as in previous games.

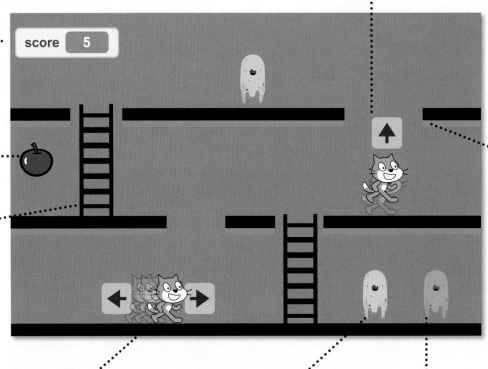

score 5

Apples will appear in random positions.

Ladders will allow the cat to climb up a floor level. Touching them will change the cat's y value by 1, moving it up automatically.

Turquoise-coloured ceilings will stop the cat climbing up, unless there is a gap.

The left and right arrow keys will change the cat's x value, making it move.

Ghost sprites will move around the house. If they touch the player then it's game over.

Ghosts will have a random amount of transparency, making them flicker.

create a new file.

2 Prepare the background

Select the stage that so we can draw a background.

Stage
Backdrops

Click the **Stage** icon.

🖌 **Backdrops**

Click the **Backdrops** tab.

🖼 **Convert to Bitmap**

Click the **Convert to Bitmap** button.

3 Darkness

Make a dark grey backdrop.

Pick the **Fill** tool.

Pick a dark grey colour.

| 0 |
| 0 |
| 32 |

Fill the backdrop.

4 Draw four floors

Draw the floors. Remember, the colours will tell our code how things work, so keep to black. You can add extra details later.

Select the **Rectangle** tool.

Make the floors black.

| 0 |
| 0 |
| 0 |

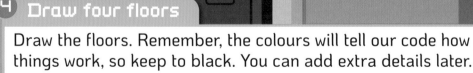

If things go wrong, click Undo.

Draw four quite thin rectangles across the stage. The bottom one should be right at the bottom. The top floor doesn't need to have quite as much space as the others.

5 Add the ceilings

Our code will need to know if the player is touching the floor or the ceiling, so we need to make the ceiling a different colour.

Mix a turquoise colour.

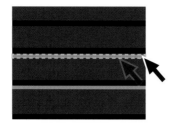

Draw ceilings underneath the top three floors. They need to be slightly thinner than the black floors.

6 Get grey

We need to make some gaps for the ladders and for the cat to jump through. The eraser would rub out all the colours, so we will paint over part of each floor with dark grey.

This method gives us exactly the correct shade of grey we used before.

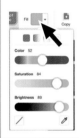

Click the colour menu.

Select the Pipette.

Click to choose dark grey.

7 Make the gaps

Now, use the Rectangle tool to draw six grey rectangles over the floors and ceilings.

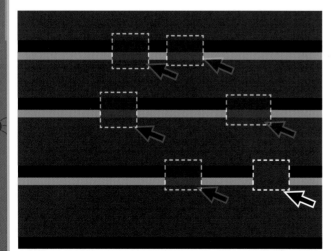

Your stage should end up like this. Use the correct colours so that the code will work properly.

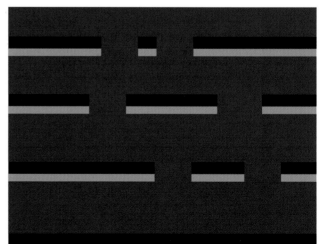

Draw a ladder on each floor so that the cat will be able to climb up through one of the gaps.

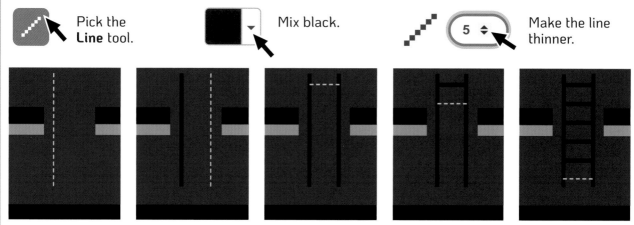

Pick the **Line** tool.

Mix black.

Make the line thinner.

Use the Line tool to gradually build up a ladder. Don't worry if your ladder is a bit wonky. It is meant to be a haunted house! Use the **Undo** button if you make a mistake when you're drawing.

9 Check

Your drawing area should look roughly like this.

Worried about giant cats? Don't panic! The cat will be much smaller when we start coding it.

If you get really stuck you can download the backdrop from thequestkids.com or maxw.com

10 Add a sprite

We will start by adding ghost sprites.

 Click the **Choose a Sprite** button.

11 Grab a ghost

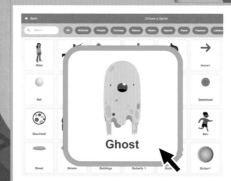

Ghost

Scroll through the sprites and click on **Ghost**.

12 Code the ghost

Add this code to get the ghost ready and to check if it has hit something.

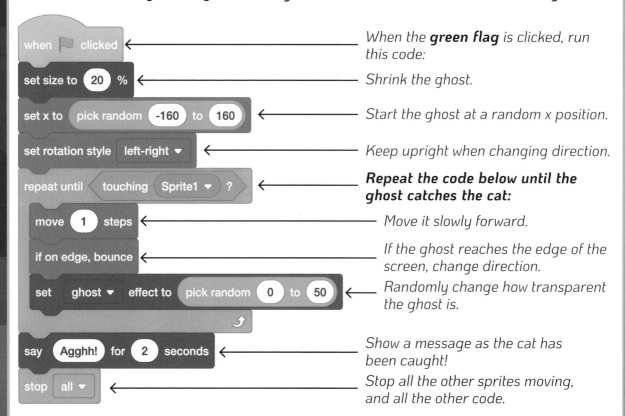

when ⚑ clicked — *When the **green flag** is clicked, run this code:*

set size to 20 % — *Shrink the ghost.*

set x to pick random -160 to 160 — *Start the ghost at a random x position.*

set rotation style left-right ▼ — *Keep upright when changing direction.*

repeat until touching Sprite1 ▼ ? — ***Repeat the code below until the ghost catches the cat:***

move 1 steps — *Move it slowly forward.*

if on edge, bounce — *If the ghost reaches the edge of the screen, change direction.*

set ghost ▼ effect to pick random 0 to 50 — *Randomly change how transparent the ghost is.*

say Agghh! for 2 seconds — *Show a message as the cat has been caught!*

stop all ▼ — *Stop all the other sprites moving, and all the other code.*

⚑ Test out the code. The ghost should move across the stage, going from side to side until it hits the cat.

USING THE COLOUR EFFECT BLOCK

set color ▼ effect to 0

This is a great block for creating special colour effects.

set color ▼ effect to 0
- color
- fisheye
- whirl
- pixelate
- mosaic
- brightness
- ghost

Click on the drop-down then choose the effect you want.

set ghost ▼ effect to 0

Type in a number between 0 and 100 to show how strong you want the effect to be — e.g. setting the ghost effect to 50 will make a sprite half-transparent.

13 Another ghost

Once the ghost is working okay, we can make another one.

 Click the ghost sprite icon with the **right mouse** button.

 Click **duplicate**.

 Another ghost should appear next to the first one.

When you duplicate a sprite, all of its code gets duplicated too!

🏳 Run your code again. The second ghost should start moving.

That's handy!

14 And another!

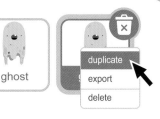

Repeat Step 13 to make another ghost. You need five or six ghosts in total.

15 Spread out the ghosts

Put one or two ghosts on each floor.

🏳 Try out the code. Each ghost should jump to a new random position on its floor, and slowly start moving along.

USING THE PICK RANDOM BLOCK

This block is used to send other blocks a random number.

*Drag the **pick random** block over a block you want to randomise.*

Drop it in place.

Choose the range of numbers you want:

Smallest number   Largest number

16 Select the cat

We need to code the cat next, so click on it to select it.

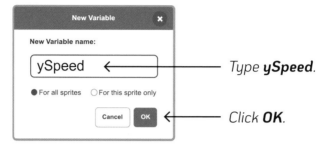

17 Add the speed variable

To store how fast the cat is moving up or down, make a variable called ySpeed.

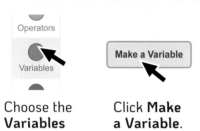

Choose the **Variables** group.

Click **Make a Variable**.

New Variable

New Variable name:

ySpeed ← — Type **ySpeed**.

● For all sprites ○ For this sprite only

Cancel OK ← — Click **OK**.

18 Cat code

Add these blocks to get the cat ready and to make it move left and right.

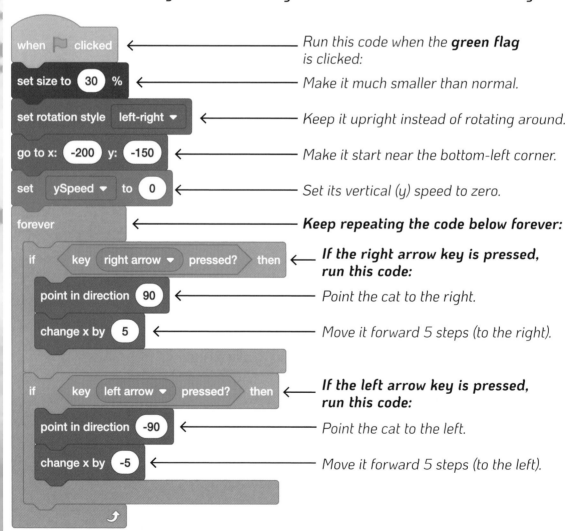

```
when [green flag] clicked        ← Run this code when the green flag is clicked:
set size to 30 %                 ← Make it much smaller than normal.
set rotation style left-right ▼  ← Keep it upright instead of rotating around.
go to x: -200 y: -150            ← Make it start near the bottom-left corner.
set ySpeed ▼ to 0                ← Set its vertical (y) speed to zero.
forever                          ← Keep repeating the code below forever:
  if < key right arrow ▼ pressed? > then   ← If the right arrow key is pressed, run this code:
    point in direction 90        ← Point the cat to the right.
    change x by 5                ← Move it forward 5 steps (to the right).

  if < key left arrow ▼ pressed? > then    ← If the left arrow key is pressed, run this code:
    point in direction -90       ← Point the cat to the left.
    change x by -5               ← Move it forward 5 steps (to the left).
```

Check your code works. Move the cat left and right with the arrow keys.

19 Up and down

Add the code below to allow the cat to move up and down.

blocks first.

```
when [flag] clicked
forever
    change y by ySpeed
    if < touching color [black] ? > then
        set ySpeed to 1
        if < key up arrow pressed? > then
            set ySpeed to 8
    else
        change ySpeed by -0.5
        if < touching color [white] ? > then
            set ySpeed to -1
```

Run the code below when the **green flag** is clicked:

Keep repeating the code below forever:
*Change the y value of the cat by the value stored in the **ySpeed** variable.*

If it hits the floor or ladder, run this code:
← Use the Pipette.

Set ySpeed to 1, making it bounce up by a very small amount.

If the up arrow key is pressed then run this:

Make the cat move up quickly.

Else it is in the air, so run this code:

Change the ySpeed variable by -0.5, making it gradually accelerate back down.

If the cat hits the ceiling then run this:

Make the cat start moving back down.

Test your code. Use the arrow keys to move left or right, and the up arrow key to jump. Check the automatic ladders are working. But watch out for the ghosts.

20 Starting note

We will add some spooky music in a moment. We will need a variable to store the starting note.

Operators

Variables

Choose the **Variables** group.

Make a Variable

Click **Make a Variable**.

New Variable

New Variable name:

| Note |

● For all sprites ○ For this sprite only

Cancel **OK**

*Type **Note**.*

*Click **OK**.*

21 Import the music blocks

There are already some blocks in Scratch to play sound effects, but we will extend this by adding some extra music blocks.

Click the **Add Extension** button (in the bottom left of the screen).

Choose the **Music** extension.

22 Spooky tune

Add these blocks to play some spooky music in the background.

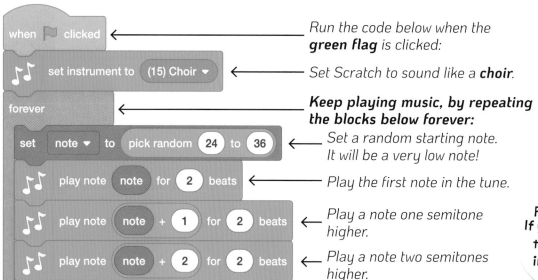

Run the code below when the ***green flag*** *is clicked:*

*Set Scratch to sound like a **choir**.*

Keep playing music, by repeating the blocks below forever:

Set a random starting note. It will be a very low note!

Play the first note in the tune.

Play a note one semitone higher.

Play a note two semitones higher.

Play the last note in the tune.

Some computers play sound differently. If you can't hear anything, try setting a different instrument (and check your volume!).

Run your code and you should hear a spooky tune play in the background!

23 Add a sprite

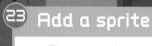

Click **Choose a Sprite**.

24 Pick an apple

Click on the **Apple** sprite.

Add a variable to keep count of how many apples get eaten.

Click **Make a Variable**.

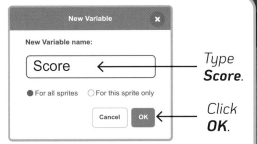

Type **Score**.

Click **OK**.

26 Spooky tune

This code will position the apples randomly and check how many get eaten.

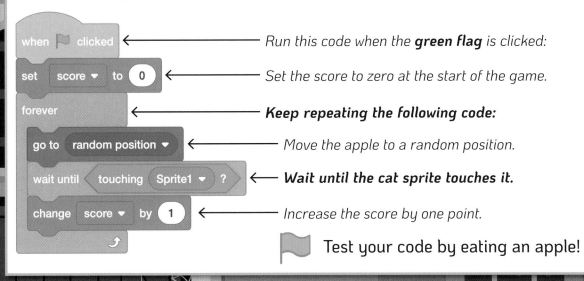

when ⚑ clicked ⟵ — *Run this code when the **green flag** is clicked:*

set score to 0 ⟵ — *Set the score to zero at the start of the game.*

forever ⟵ — **Keep repeating the following code:**

go to random position ⟵ — *Move the apple to a random position.*

wait until < touching Sprite1 ? ⟵ — **Wait until the cat sprite touches it.**

change score by 1 ⟵ — *Increase the score by one point.*

⚑ Test your code by eating an apple!

27 More apples

Right-click on the **Apple** sprite.

Choose **duplicate** to add another apple. Add one more to make three.

28 Play the game!

⚑ Now, try playing your game! How many apples can you eat before the ghosts get you?

Spooky!

Challenges

- Make all the apples smaller.
- Draw some things in the background of the house – maybe some cobwebs and a skeleton?
- Change how fast the ghosts move around.
- Add some other objects to collect. How many points will they be worth?
- Experiment with the background music. Can you make it even spookier?
- Make the ghosts change direction more often.

Scrolling Platform

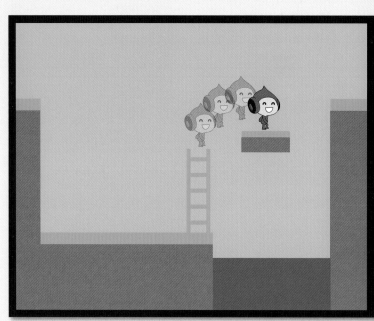

In this game Pico has to complete a series of challenges, leaping from platform to platform. As each one is completed, the next challenge – or level – will scroll across the screen. This is coded by using separate sprites for each level. A scrollX variable will keep track of the player's progress. Jumping up and down will work in a similar way to previous games. Additional colours will create extra hazards for the player.

HOW THE GAME WORKS

The scrollX variable will store how far through the game the player is.

The player doesn't actually move left or right. Pressing the arrow keys changes the scrollX variable, making the platforms scroll sideways.

The ySpeed variable will control how fast Pico moves up or down – the same way as in previous games.

scrollX   -120

Anything drawn in red on one of the sprites will end the game for Pico!

Green and brown colours will be used to tell Pico what is a wall and what is safe to stand on.

If Pico falls out of the stage then it's game over.

Each level in the game is designed on a separate sprite.
The sprites all scroll left as Pico moves through the game.

Sprite1   Sprite2   Sprite3   Sprite4

1 Start Scratch

Go to the Scratch website and create a new file.

scratch.mit.edu

2 Delete the cat

We don't need the cat so click on the bin to delete it.

Sprite1

3 Prepare the background

Get the background ready for drawing.

✏ Backdrops

🖼 Convert to Bitmap

Click the **Backdrops** tab.

Click **Convert to Bitmap**.

4 Draw the sky

Make a blue sky.

53
68
100

Pick the **Fill** tool.

Mix a blue colour.

Fill the sky in blue.

Don't draw anything else on the backdrop.

Whee!

5 Add a sprite

Next, we need to add the main player sprite.

Click **Choose a Sprite**.

In the other games, we have drawn platforms on the backdrop. In this game, the platforms need to scroll, so they will be drawn on sprites instead.

6 Find Pico Walking

Pico Walking

Scroll through the sprites and click on the **Pico Walking** sprite.

7 Add the scroll variable

The game will need a variable to store how far the platform sprites need to scroll sideways. We will call it **scrollX**.

Operators

Variables

Make a Variable

Choose the **Variables** group.

Click **Make a Variable**.

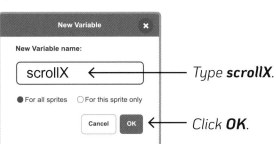

New Variable

New Variable name:

scrollX ← — *Type **scrollX**.*

● For all sprites   ○ For this sprite only

Cancel   OK ← — *Click **OK**.*

8 Add the speed variable

To store how fast Pico is moving up or down, make a second variable called ySpeed.

Make a Variable

Click **Make a Variable**.

New Variable

New Variable name:

ySpeed ← *Type **ySpeed**.*

● For all sprites ○ For this sprite only

Cancel **OK** ← *Click **OK**.*

How do I get down?

9 Start coding Pico

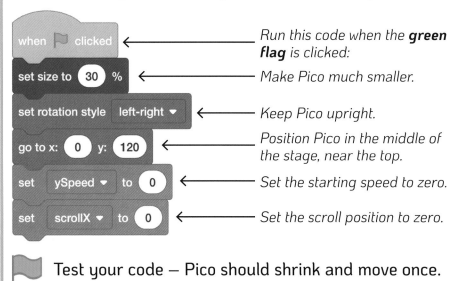

This code will get Pico ready at the start of the game.

when 🚩 clicked	*Run this code when the **green flag** is clicked:*
set size to 30 %	*Make Pico much smaller.*
set rotation style left-right ▼	*Keep Pico upright.*
go to x: 0 y: 120	*Position Pico in the middle of the stage, near the top.*
set ySpeed ▼ to 0	*Set the starting speed to zero.*
set scrollX ▼ to 0	*Set the scroll position to zero.*

🚩 Test your code – Pico should shrink and move once.

10 Add a painted sprite

Add a sprite to contain the platforms for the first level of your game.

Hover

Move your mouse to **hover** over the **Choose a Sprite** button.

Don't click it!

Paint

A menu like this will appear.

Move your mouse up to the **Paint** option and click it.

11 Bitmap

Convert to Bitmap

Click the **Convert to Bitmap** button.

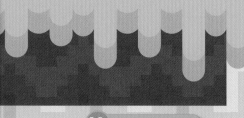

46

12 Draw a simple platform

Draw a simple rectangle to be the ground in the first level.

 Select the **Rectangle** tool.

Mix a brown colour for the ground.

9
60
78

Draw a rectangle across the drawing area.

13 Add some grass

Draw another green rectangle on top of the ground.

 Make a green colour.

39
84
85

Draw a thinner rectangle on top.

14 Code the sprite

 Code

Click the **Code** tab and add this code. The level just needs a short bit of code to make it scroll to the correct place.

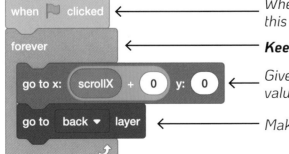

*When the **green flag** is clicked, run this code:*

Keep looping this code forever:

Give this sprite an x value equal to the value of scrollX, and a y value of zero.

Make sure the sprite is behind Pico.

 Run your code. All that will happen is that the platform should snap to the bottom of the stage.

Pico Walking

Select Pico by clicking the Pico sprite icon.

Now, it's time to get the arrow keys working. As the code is quite complex, we'll split the left and right arrow keys into two sections. Add this code to deal with moving right:

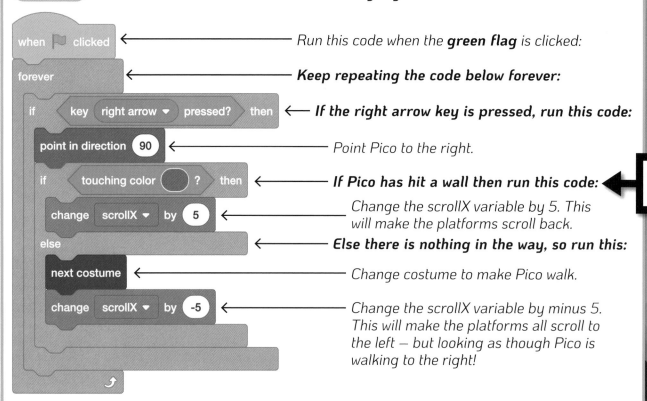

when ⚑ clicked ← *Run this code when the **green flag** is clicked:*

forever ← ***Keep repeating the code below forever:***

if key right arrow ▾ pressed? then ← ***If the right arrow key is pressed, run this code:***

point in direction 90 ← *Point Pico to the right.*

if touching color ? then ← ***If Pico has hit a wall then run this code:***

change scrollX ▾ by 5 ← *Change the scrollX variable by 5. This will make the platforms scroll back.*

else ← ***Else there is nothing in the way, so run this:***

next costume ← *Change costume to make Pico walk.*

change scrollX ▾ by -5 ← *Change the scrollX variable by minus 5. This will make the platforms all scroll to the left — but looking as though Pico is walking to the right!*

⚑ Check your code works. Press the right arrow key, and Pico's legs should start moving. The platform should gradually slide left.

> Once you have the move-right code working you could duplicate it.

DUPLICATING CODE BLOCKS

We've seen how to duplicate sprites, but it's also possible to duplicate sections of code.

This is worth doing if you need to make two very similar sections of code.

For example, imagine you have made some code that moves a sprite to the right. You have tested it and it works okay.

You now need a very similar piece of code to make the sprite move to the left. Instead of building it block by block you can duplicate the first section of code, then adapt it to make the sprite move left.

Right-click *your mouse on the first block of code in the section.*

Duplicate
Add Comment
Delete Block

A menu should appear.
*Click **Duplicate**.*

Drag the new duplicated code to some empty space and click to place it.

*Make **all** the changes you need to your new section of code.*

And now, the opposite for the left arrow key. Add this code:

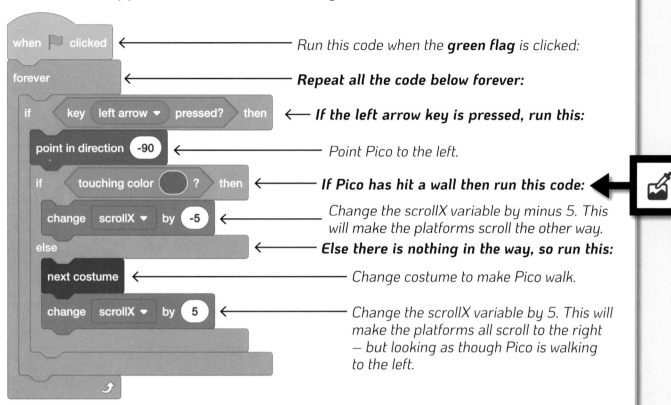

when ⚑ clicked ⟵ ——————— *Run this code when the **green flag** is clicked:*

forever ⟵ ——————— **Repeat all the code below forever:**

if key left arrow ▾ pressed? then ⟵— **If the left arrow key is pressed, run this:**

point in direction -90 ⟵———— *Point Pico to the left.*

if touching color ⬤ ? then ⟵— **If Pico has hit a wall then run this code:**

change scrollX ▾ by -5 ⟵—— *Change the scrollX variable by minus 5. This will make the platforms scroll the other way.*

else ⟵———— **Else there is nothing in the way, so run this:**

next costume ⟵———— *Change costume to make Pico walk.*

change scrollX ▾ by 5 ⟵———— *Change the scrollX variable by 5. This will make the platforms all scroll to the right — but looking as though Pico is walking to the left.*

⚑ Test your code. Press the left arrow key and the platform should gradually slide right. Try going backwards and forwards.

If your code doesn't work properly, check you have put 5 and –5 in the correct places.

Hmm...

17 Up and down

Add the code to handle moving up and down. It's similar to the code in the other platform games we've made.

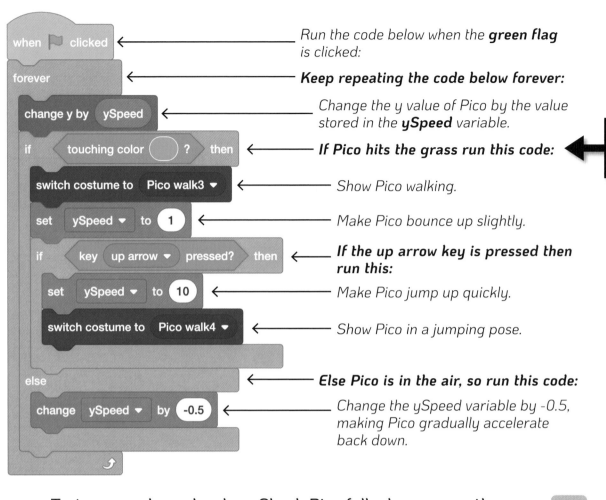

Run the code below when the **green flag** is clicked:

Keep repeating the code below forever:

Change the y value of Pico by the value stored in the **ySpeed** variable.

If Pico hits the grass run this code:

Show Pico walking.

Make Pico bounce up slightly.

If the up arrow key is pressed then run this:

Make Pico jump up quickly.

Show Pico in a jumping pose.

Else Pico is in the air, so run this code:

Change the ySpeed variable by -0.5, making Pico gradually accelerate back down.

🚩 Test your code works okay. Check Pico falls down correctly. If you press the up arrow key, Pico should jump up.

18 Another level

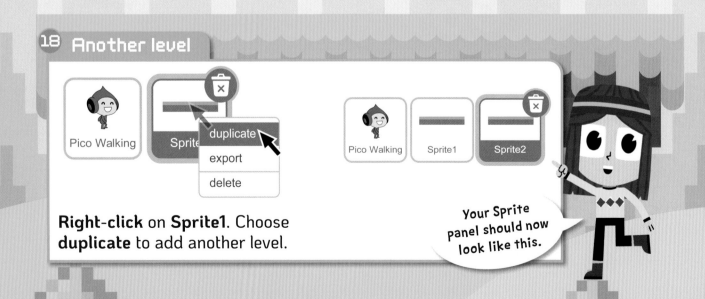

Right-click on **Sprite1**. Choose **duplicate** to add another level.

Your Sprite panel should now look like this.

19

Start editing

Now, start designing the new level.

Click the **Costumes** tab.

Use the Pipette to get the exact brown used for the ground:

Click the Colour menu.

Select the Pipette.

Click the ground.

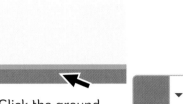

This method gives us exactly the same shade of brown we used before.

Click Undo if you make a mistake.

---

20 **Design the level**

Use the Rectangle tool to create the level.

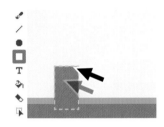

Draw a rectangle on top of the ground.

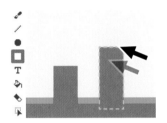

Draw another rectangle.

Use the Pipette to get the green colour.

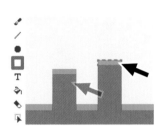

Add some grass on top of both rectangles.

---

21 **Code the new sprite**

 Code

Click the **Code** tab and *edit* the code so that it looks like this. It will make sure the new sprite scrolls into place next to the first one.

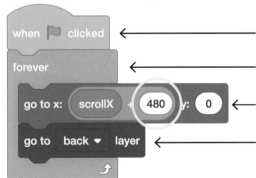

*When the **flag** is clicked, run this code:*

Repeat this code forever:

*Give this sprite an x value **480** pixels further to the right than the first platform sprite.*

Make sure the platform sprite is behind Pico.

Test your code. As you press the right arrow key, your new platform sprite should gradually scroll into view!

We use 480 because that's the width of the stage and of each platform sprite.

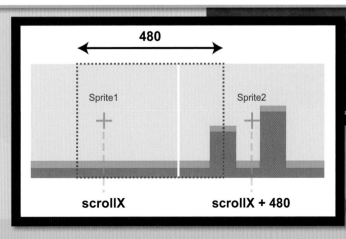

22 And another sprite!

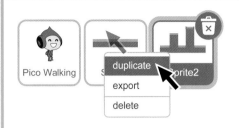

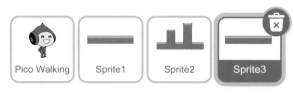

This is how your Sprite panel should look now.

Right-click on **Sprite1**.
Choose **duplicate**.

Use the Pipette tool to get the exact shade of green and brown.

23 Edit Sprite3's costume

Click the **Costumes** tab, then change the costume to look like this:

Use the Rectangle tool to make all the shapes.

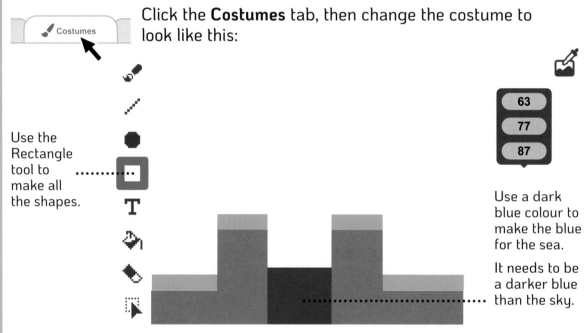

63
77
87

Use a dark blue colour to make the blue for the sea.

It needs to be a darker blue than the sky.

24 Code the new sprite

Click the **Code** tab then edit the code. You should only need to change the number in the green block to make it scroll correctly.

These blocks should be here already.

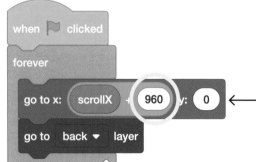

when ▶ clicked

forever

go to x: scrollX + 960 y: 0

go to back ▼ layer

*Give this sprite an x value **960** pixels further to the right than the first platform sprite.*

After you add a new part to your game you need to try it. It needs to be hard – but not impossible! You may have to go back and make the gap smaller by adding more green grass.

🚩 Test your code. Try moving around and try out the new platform. What happens if you land in the water?

25 Falling out

If Pico falls down to the bottom of the screen we need the game to end. Add this code:

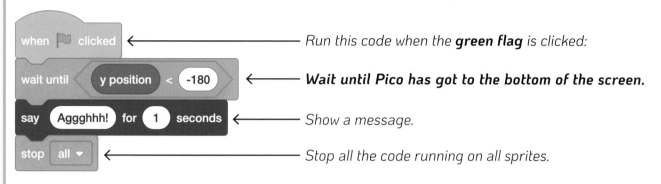

when ⚑ clicked ⟵———————————— *Run this code when the **green flag** is clicked:*

wait until (y position < -180) ⟵——— ***Wait until Pico has got to the bottom of the screen.***

say (Aggghhh!) for (1) seconds ⟵——— *Show a message.*

stop (all ▾) ⟵—————————————— *Stop all the code running on all sprites.*

⚑ Test your code. Try falling in the water again — the game should end. Try jumping off the end of the platform and check that the game ends too.

26 Other hazards!

We will add some other hazards now — some deadly spikes!

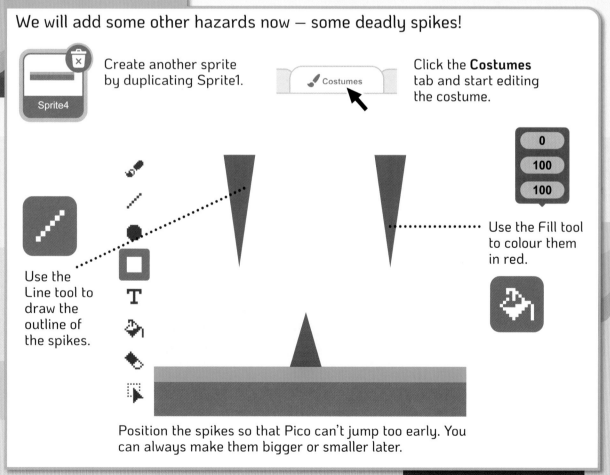

Create another sprite by duplicating Sprite1.

Sprite4

Click the **Costumes** tab and start editing the costume.

Costumes

0
100
100

Use the Fill tool to colour them in red.

Use the Line tool to draw the outline of the spikes.

Position the spikes so that Pico can't jump too early. You can always make them bigger or smaller later.

27 Code the spiky sprite

Click the **Code** tab and edit the code to make the spiky sprite scroll correctly.

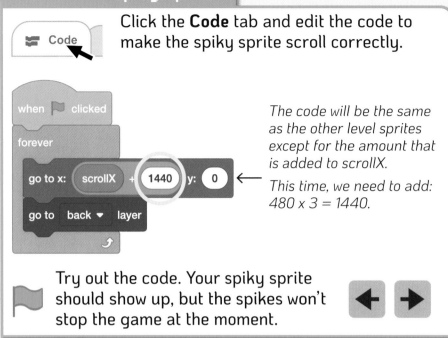

The code will be the same as the other level sprites except for the amount that is added to scrollX.

This time, we need to add: 480 x 3 = 1440.

Try out the code. Your spiky sprite should show up, but the spikes won't stop the game at the moment.

ADDING MORE LEVELS

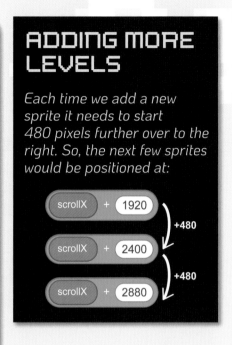

Each time we add a new sprite it needs to start 480 pixels further over to the right. So, the next few sprites would be positioned at:

scrollX + 1920
+480
scrollX + 2400
+480
scrollX + 2880

28 Check for spikes

Select Pico by clicking the Pico Walking sprite icon.

We need to add code to check for spikes.

You need to select the sprite you are adding code to. It needs to be Pico!

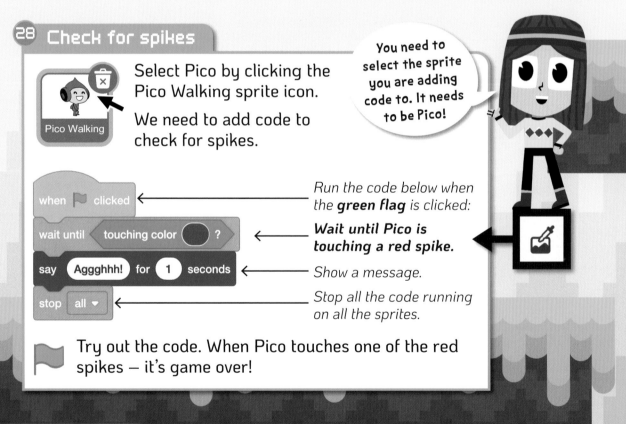

Run the code below when the **green flag** is clicked:

Wait until Pico is touching a red spike.

Show a message.

Stop all the code running on all the sprites.

Try out the code. When Pico touches one of the red spikes — it's game over!

29 Add more sprites

Now, it's time for you to let your imagination run wild as you design extra challenges for Pico! Just keep following the steps you used to make the other sprites:

Duplicate Sprite1.

Use the exact colours!

Draw the costume.

Change this value.

Edit the code.

Challenges

Can you create these platforms?

Green ladders will be climbed automatically!

Other colours will be treated as the background and will be ignored by Pico.

Function Freddie

In this game our player, Function Freddie, has to jump from platform to platform across multiple levels. You will build this game by creating your own code blocks. Coders sometimes call this "creating your own functions". This will be slightly more complex than the other coding we have done so far. But making your own blocks will give you a set of code blocks that you can reuse to build other platform games.

HOW THE GAME WORKS

The ySpeed variable will work in a similar way to previous games.

A new level will be started when the player reaches the orange door.

level 1

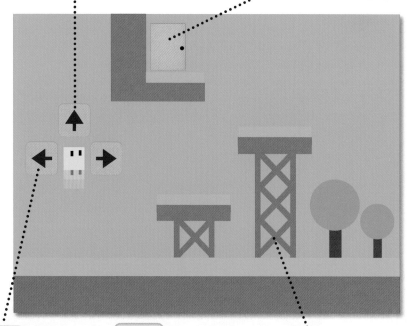

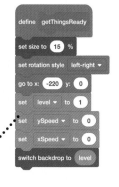

Blocks will be created to make different parts of the game work.

xSpeed

The xSpeed variable will give the player a smoother sideways movement.

Each level is stored as a different backdrop.

Light green and brown colours will stop the player moving. The other colours are just part of the background.

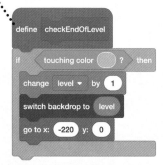

Code will define how each of the new blocks work.

1 Start Scratch

Go to the Scratch website and create a new file.

scratch.mit.edu

2 Delete the cat

We won't need the cat so click on the bin to delete it.

Sprite1

3 Add a painted sprite

Add a sprite to make your player.

Hover

Move your mouse to *hover* over the **Choose a Sprite** button.

Don't click it!

Paint

A menu like this will appear.

Move your mouse up to the **Paint** option and click it.

4 Bitmap

Click the **Convert to Bitmap** button.

Click Undo if things go wrong.

5 Draw the player sprite

Draw a simple box with eyes, to be the player sprite.

Select the **Rectangle** tool.

Mix a yellow colour.

| 18 |
| 91 |
| 100 |

Draw a square about half the height of the drawing area.

Make black.

| 0 |
| 0 |
| 0 |

Add two more rectangles, to be the eyes.

6 Rename the sprite

It will make our code easier if we rename the sprite as **player**.

Sprite player ← *Type* **player**.

player

Nice!

7 Add the ySpeed variable

To store how fast the player is moving up or down, make a variable called **ySpeed**.

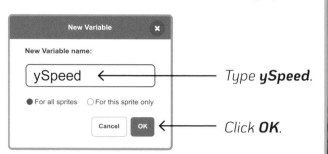

Click the **Code** tab.

Choose the **Variables** group.

Click **Make a Variable**.

New Variable
New Variable name:
ySpeed
● For all sprites ○ For this sprite only
Cancel OK

*Type **ySpeed**.*

*Click **OK**.*

8 Add an xSpeed variable

In this game we are also going to store how fast the player moves left or right, so make a variable called **xSpeed**.

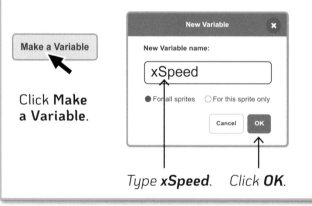

Click **Make a Variable**.

*Type **xSpeed**.* *Click **OK**.*

9 Add a level variable

We also need to store the current game level. Make another variable called **level**.

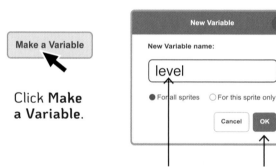

Click **Make a Variable**.

*Type **level**.* *Click **OK**.*

10 Make a new block

We are going to be making our own function blocks in this game. To start with we'll make a block called **getThingsReady**. It will get everything ready before the game starts.

Choose the **My Blocks** group.

Click **Make a Block**.

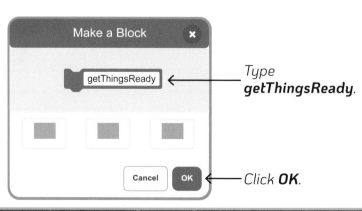

*Type **getThingsReady**.*

*Click **OK**.*

When you are making your own blocks it's a good idea to name them in a way that describes what they do.

Most coding languages don't let you type a space within a function name. So, coders use capital letters to start each word in a function name. This is called camel case because it looks like a camel with lots of humps!

58

getThingsReady

Our brand new block should have appeared under the **Make a Block** button. But if we use the new block, it won't do anything yet.

We need to explain to Scratch what the **getThingsReady** block should do. Add this code:

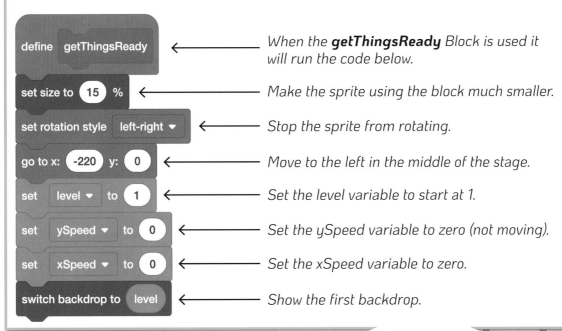

← *When the **getThingsReady** Block is used it will run the code below.*

← *Make the sprite using the block much smaller.*

← *Stop the sprite from rotating.*

← *Move to the left in the middle of the stage.*

← *Set the level variable to start at 1.*

← *Set the ySpeed variable to zero (not moving).*

← *Set the xSpeed variable to zero.*

← *Show the first backdrop.*

> There's no point running your code yet. But go back and carefully check you entered it all correctly.

12 Prepare the background

Select the stage so that we can draw a background.

Click the **Stage** icon.

 Backdrops

Click the **Backdrops** tab.

 Convert to Bitmap

Click the **Convert to Bitmap** button.

13 Draw the sky

Draw a blue sky.

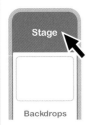

Pick the **Fill** tool.

Mix a blue colour.

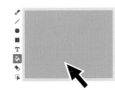

54
60
100

Fill the sky in blue.

14 Draw a simple platform

Draw a simple rectangle to be the ground in the first level.

 Select the **Rectangle** tool.

Make a brown colour for the ground.

11
60
60

Draw a rectangle across the drawing area.

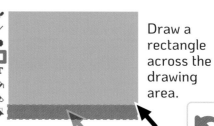
If things go wrong then click Undo.

15 Add some grass

Now, draw some grass.

Mix a green colour.

34
60
78

Draw a thin green rectangle on top.

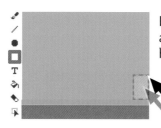
In "Monkey City" we checked the x value to check when a level was completed. Using a door like this means we can position the end of level anywhere on each backdrop.

16 Draw a door

The player will need to reach a door to progress to the next level. Draw a simple orange door.

Make orange.

11
83
100

Draw the door at the right-hand side.

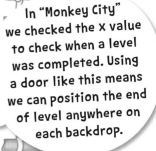
Use the **Circle** tool to add a small, black handle.

17 Select the player

 Click the player sprite to select it.

player

Now, make a block to deal with moving up or down.

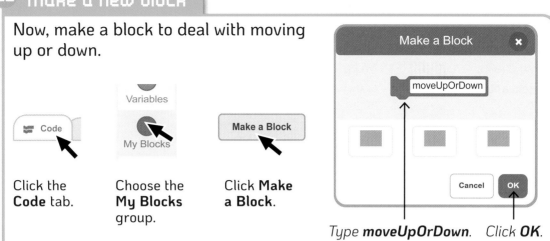

Make a Block

moveUpOrDown

Cancel   OK

Click the **Code** tab.

Choose the **My Blocks** group.

Click **Make a Block**.

Type **moveUpOrDown**.   Click **OK**.

Now, we need to define what the **moveUpOrDown** block will do. Add the code below:

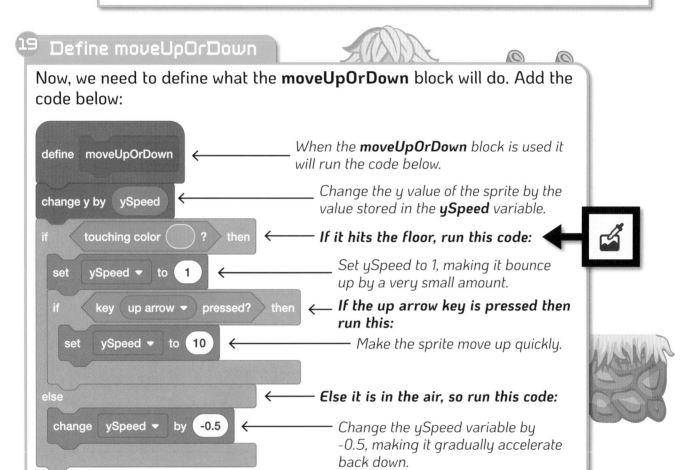

define moveUpOrDown ← *When the **moveUpOrDown** block is used it will run the code below.*

change y by ySpeed ← *Change the y value of the sprite by the value stored in the **ySpeed** variable.*

if touching color ( ) ? then ← **If it hits the floor, run this code:**

set ySpeed ▾ to 1 ← *Set ySpeed to 1, making it bounce up by a very small amount.*

if key up arrow ▾ pressed? then ← **If the up arrow key is pressed then run this:**

set ySpeed ▾ to 10 ← *Make the sprite move up quickly.*

else ← **Else it is in the air, so run this code:**

change ySpeed ▾ by -0.5 ← *Change the ySpeed variable by -0.5, making it gradually accelerate back down.*

So that we can test out the new blocks, add some blocks that use them:

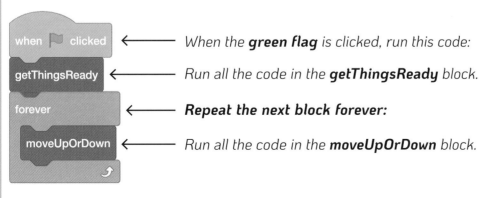

when ⚑ clicked ← *When the **green flag** is clicked, run this code:*

getThingsReady ← *Run all the code in the **getThingsReady** block.*

forever ← **Repeat the next block forever:**

moveUpOrDown ← *Run all the code in the **moveUpOrDown** block.*

⚑ Try the code so far. The player should fall down and bounce. If you press the up arrow it should jump back up.

20

Make a new block

Now, make a block to manage moving left or right.

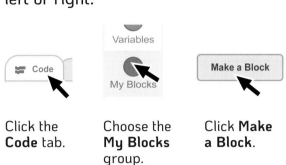

Click the **Code** tab.

Choose the **My Blocks** group.

Click **Make a Block**.

Make a Block

moveLeftOrRight

Cancel   OK

*Type **moveLeftOrRight**.   Click **OK**.*

Define moveLeftOrRight

Add some code to define what the **moveLeftOrRight** block will do.

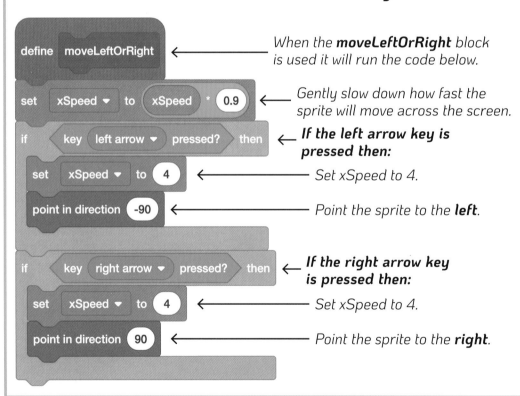

define moveLeftOrRight ← *When the **moveLeftOrRight** block is used it will run the code below.*

set xSpeed ▾ to (xSpeed * 0.9) ← *Gently slow down how fast the sprite will move across the screen.*

if (key left arrow ▾ pressed?) then ← ***If the left arrow key is pressed then:***

set xSpeed ▾ to 4 ← *Set xSpeed to 4.*

point in direction -90 ← *Point the sprite to the **left**.*

if (key right arrow ▾ pressed?) then ← ***If the right arrow key is pressed then:***

set xSpeed ▾ to 4 ← *Set xSpeed to 4.*

point in direction 90 ← *Point the sprite to the **right**.*

This block will set xSpeed and point the sprite in the correct direction. But before we actually move it, we need to check there is nothing in the way.

The next block we make needs to check if the sprite has hit the wall and then move the sprite.

Click the **Code** tab.

Choose the **My Blocks** group.

Click **Make a Block**.

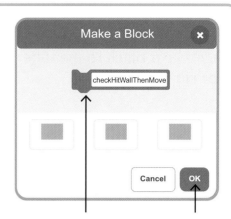

*Type **checkHitWallThenMove**. Click **OK**.*

We will need two more blocks, so let's make them now.

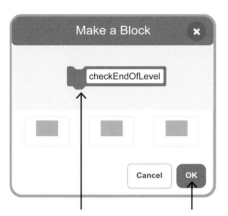

*Type **checkEndOfLevel**. Click **OK**.*

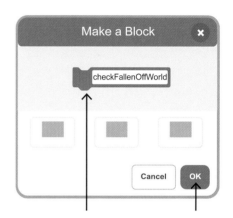

*Type **checkFallenOffWorld**. Click **OK**.*

This block needs to check it's okay to move the sprite *sideways*.
Add the code below:

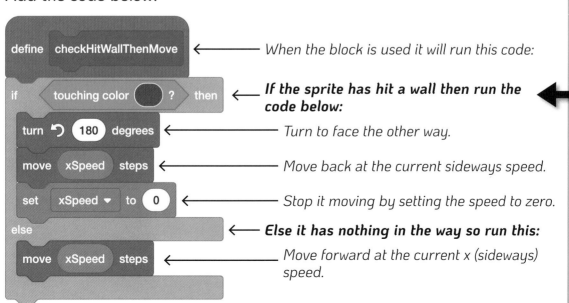

define checkHitWallThenMove ← *When the block is used it will run this code:*

if touching color ? then ← **If the sprite has hit a wall then run the code below:**

turn ↺ 180 degrees ← *Turn to face the other way.*

move xSpeed steps ← *Move back at the current sideways speed.*

set xSpeed ▼ to 0 ← *Stop it moving by setting the speed to zero.*

else ← **Else it has nothing in the way so run this:**

move xSpeed steps ← *Move forward at the current x (sideways) speed.*

We can't easily test this block yet, but check your code carefully.

24 Define checkEndOfLevel

We need this block to test if the sprite has reached a door to the next level. Add this code:

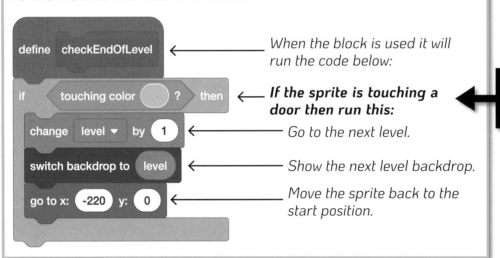

define checkEndOfLevel ← *When the block is used it will run the code below:*

if ⟨ touching color ◯ ? ⟩ then ← **If the sprite is touching a door then run this:**

change level ▾ by 1 ← *Go to the next level.*

switch backdrop to level ← *Show the next level backdrop.*

go to x: -220 y: 0 ← *Move the sprite back to the start position.*

25 Define checkFallenOffWorld

The final block needs to check the sprite hasn't fallen below the bottom of the screen.

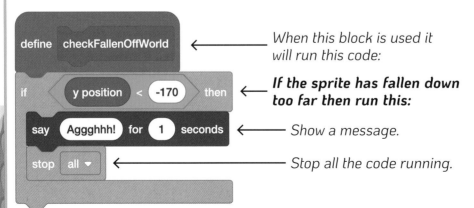

define checkFallenOffWorld ← *When this block is used it will run this code:*

if ⟨ y position < -170 ⟩ then ← **If the sprite has fallen down too far then run this:**

say Aggghhh! for 1 seconds ← *Show a message.*

stop all ▾ ← *Stop all the code running.*

26

Bring it all together

Now we have defined all the blocks, we just need to use them at the correct time. This final code will be the main part of the game and will control how everything fits together.

Find the code you started in Step 18.

Add the new blocks so that your code looks like this.

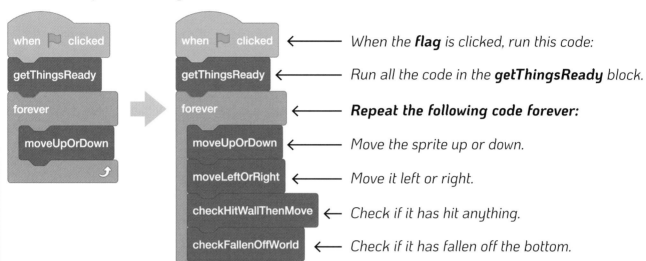

when 🚩 clicked ← *When the **flag** is clicked, run this code:*

getThingsReady ← *Run all the code in the **getThingsReady** block.*

forever ← ***Repeat the following code forever:***

moveUpOrDown ← *Move the sprite up or down.*

moveLeftOrRight ← *Move it left or right.*

checkHitWallThenMove ← *Check if it has hit anything.*

checkFallenOffWorld ← *Check if it has fallen off the bottom.*

checkEndOfLevel ← *Check if it has reached the end of the level.*

 Try out the game! You should be able to move the player around and jump up. As there is only one level, when you get to the door it will just take you back to the left side.

27

Add a backdrop

Add another backdrop to design the second level of your game.

Click the **Stage** icon.

Select the **Backdrops** tab.

Right-click the backdrop1 icon.

Click **duplicate**.

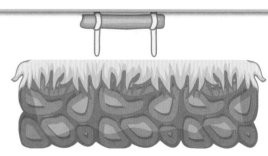

28 Edit the backdrop

Change the backdrop to look like this:

Use the Rectangle tool to make the shapes you need.

Use the Pipette tool to get the exact colour shades.

29 Add another

Duplicate another backdrop.

Right-click the backdrop1 icon.

Click **duplicate**.

30 Make some holes!

Create some holes in the ground for the player to jump over.

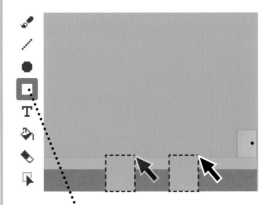

Your screen should now look like this.

Use the Rectangle tool to draw blue sky over parts of the ground.

Test your game. Try to complete each of the first three levels!

I need a break!

66

Challenges

Can you create these levels?

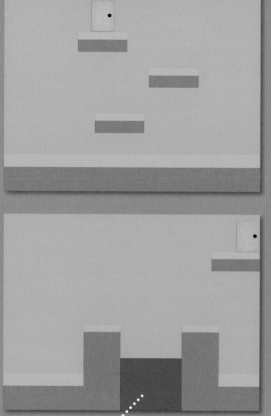

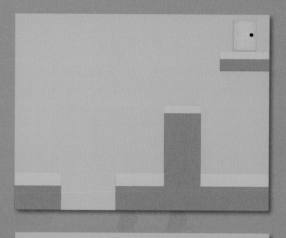

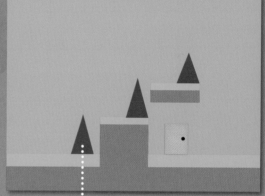

Use a different shade of blue to the sky to draw some water. Landing in it will end the game as the player will fall through it and out of the stage.

Add some red spikes. To make these game-ending, define a block that checks for red. If the player hits red then show a "game over" message and stop the code running.

Use different colours to add interesting background features to your game.

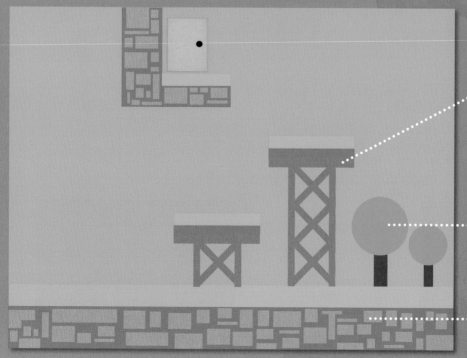

The grey girders look as though they are holding up the platforms. But because they are not one of the colours we are checking for, they will be ignored.

The trees use different shades so they will be ignored too.

Add lots of lighter rectangles to the ground to make it look like stones in a wall.

Game Challenges: Re-using your own blocks

If you have coded Function Freddie and saved your work then you are ready to use this section of the book.

moveLeftOrRight

moveUpOrDown

Once you have built your own code blocks then you can reuse them in other projects.

This will make it much quicker for you to build new games and try out new ideas.

You will need to adapt parts of the code to use them in a new game. For example, the colours your code checks for will need to be changed.

You need to have a Scratch account and be logged in to do this.

Small changes

If you are just making a slightly different version of a game you have already coded then you can just save a copy of the game, and adapt the copy.

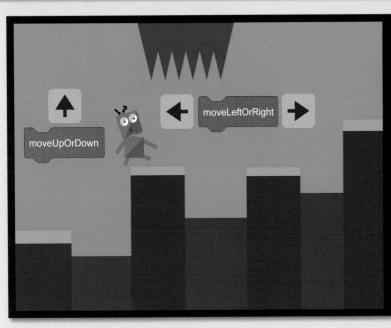

Click the **Folder** icon to load your saved files.

Find where you saved Function Freddie and click **See inside**.

Click **Save as a copy**.

Rename your project then click **File – Save now**.

For example, if you wanted to make a new version of the Haunted House game, you could save a copy of it and redesign the levels.

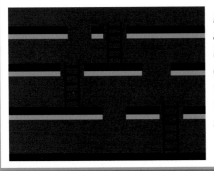

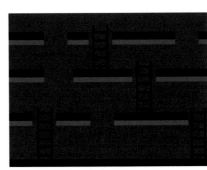

By moving the ladders and changing some of the colours you get a new game. (Some of the code would need to change, so the player sprite would stop if it hit a pink ceiling.)

There is better way to make new games that reuse your code. This is done by using the Scratch Backpack.

You probably use a real backpack to carry your books and lunch from home to school.

In Scratch you can use a special "Code Backpack" to carry code and sprites from one project to another.

USING THE BACKPACK TO MAKE NEW GAMES

If you are making a completely new game then you can still select parts of the code to reuse. This is done by putting the code you want to reuse into the Scratch **Backpack**.

ADDING CODE TO THE BACKPACK:

My Stuff

See inside

See inside

1. Open your finished Function Freddie game in one tab in your browser.

Backpack

Backpack

*2. Click **Backpack** at the bottom of the screen to open up the Code Backpack.*

Backpack

3. Drag the code you want to reuse down into the Backpack. To create the games in the final section of the book you'll need to drag in each of the seven scripts (sections) of code.

Drag each section by clicking on the first block in each section and dragging downwards.

REMOVING CODE:

Later, when you have started a new project, you can get back a copy of the code you stored in the Backpack. You just need to take it out!

Backpack

Drag the code you need out of the Backpack and drop it into your new project.

Over the next few pages you'll see some examples of how to do this to build more games!

Game Challenges: Pyramid Platform

If you have coded Function Freddie then you are ready to try making this game.

Build a new game where the cat has to make its way over a series of pyramids. The cat needs to jump over the pyramid and watch out for any hazards. When the cat finds one of the dark red rubies, it will take it to the next level.

Use the Backpack to help reuse some of the code from Function Freddie to make the game work.

You will need your own Scratch account to make the games in the challenge section of this book. See page 6 for help.

1 Sign in to Scratch

Start by going to the Scratch website.

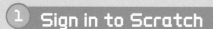
scratch.mit.edu

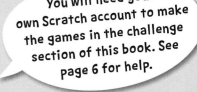

Sign in to your Scratch account.

Click **Create**.

2 Check your Backpack

At the bottom of the screen, click the Backpack. Make sure all the code from Function Freddie is in there.

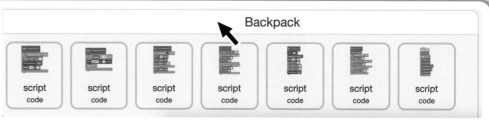

Backpack

script code | script code | script code | script code | script code | script code | script code

There should be seven icons showing seven code sections. If you can't see them, go back to page 69 for help with this.

3 Add the code from the Backpack

Drag each of the seven code sections from the Backpack up into the main code area.

This will add all the code from Function Freddie into your new game.

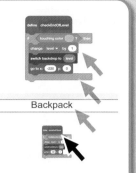

Backpack

4 Tidy up!

The code blocks will probably be piled up in a mess.

Right-click in a gap between the blocks and choose **Clean up Blocks**.

Undo
Redo
Clean up Blocks
Add Comment
Delete 61 Blocks

Your code will now be lined up neatly!

5 Prepare the background

Click the **Stage** icon.

Click the **Backdrops** tab.

Convert to Bitmap

Click the **Convert to Bitmap** button.

6 Draw the first level

Use the Rectangle tool to draw some pyramids.

(Just like real Ancient Egyptian pyramids they should be stepped, not triangular.)

The top of the Pyramids need to be a different colour for the code to work.

Use the Line and Fill tools to add a ruby at the top of the pyramid. This will be the gateway to the next level.

Colour the top of each step a lighter shade of yellow.

7 Adapt your code

Now, go through your code and make these changes so that the game works properly:

- In the **define getThingsReady** block, change the cat's size from 15% to 40%.
- In the **define moveUpOrDown** block, use the Pipette to change the colour you are sensing from dark green to the light yellow colour on top of each step of the pyramid.
- In the **define checkHitWallThenMove** block, change the colour from the brown walls in Function Freddie to the main yellow colour of the pyramids.
- In the **define checkEndOfLevel** block, make sure the orange colour is changed to the red colour of the ruby at the end of each level.

 Test your code. If you have problems, check you added all seven code sections from the Backpack and that the colours are all set correctly. Then, design some more levels for your game!

Game Challenges: Crazy Castle

If you have coded Function Freddie then you are ready to try making this game.

Create a game where a knight has to move around a crazy castle. Each level is made of different parts of the castle. The knight can jump onto walls and climb up towers. Reaching a door takes the knight onto the next level.

Reuse some of the code from Function Freddie to make the different parts of the game work.

1 Sign in to Scratch

Start by going to the Scratch website and signing in to your account. Click **Create**.

Sign in

2 Check your Backpack

Make sure all the code from Function Freddie is in the Backpack. There should be seven icons showing seven code sections. If you can't see them, go back to page 69 for help with this.

3 Delete the cat

Click on the bin to delete the cat.

Sprite1

4 Add a sprite

Add the main player sprite.

Click **Choose a Sprite**.

5 Find the knight

Scroll through the sprites and click on the **Knight** sprite.

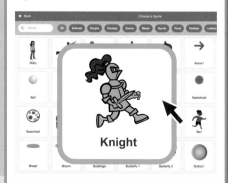

6 Add the code from the Backpack

Drag each of the seven code sections from the Backpack up into the main code area.

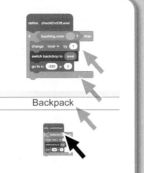

This will add all the code from Function Freddie into your new game.

7 Tidy up!

The code blocks will probably be piled up in a mess.

Right-click in a gap between the blocks and choose **Clean up Blocks**.

Your code will now be lined up neatly!

8 Prepare the background

 Click the **Stage** icon.

 Click the **Backdrops** tab.

 Click the **Convert to Bitmap** button.

9 Draw the first level

Use the drawing tools to draw a castle for the Knight sprite to explore.

Use the different shape tools to make your background. Look back through the book for help.

You can draw quite a simple background to start with and add more details later.

Make sure the colour of the battlements at the top of the castle is a different grey from the main castle walls.

10 Adapt your code

Go through your code and make these changes that so the game works properly:
- In the **define getThingsReady** block, change the size from 15% to around 40%.
- In the **define moveUpOrDown** block, use the Pipette to change the colour you are sensing from dark green to the light colour used in the castle battlements.
- In the **define checkHitWallThenMove** block, change the colour from brown to the dark grey of the castle walls.
- In the **define checkEndOfLevel** block, make sure the orange colour is changed to the exact shade of the door you have drawn.

 Test your code. If you have problems, check you added all seven code sections from the Backpack and that the colours are all set correctly. Then, make some more levels for your game!

Game Challenges: Robot Runner

Wait until you have coded Function Freddie and it is working before making this game!

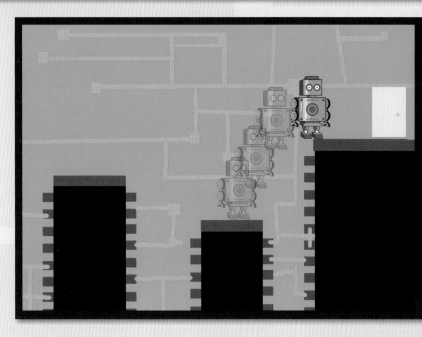

In this game a minature robot has to make his way through an enormous computer. The platforms in the game will be different microchips inside the computer.

We will reuse some of the code from Function Freddie to make the different parts of the game work.

1 Sign in to Scratch

Go to the Scratch website and sign in to your account. Click **Create**.

2 Check your Backpack

Make sure all the code from Function Freddie is in the Backpack. There should be seven icons showing seven code sections. If you can't see them, go back to page 69 for help with this.

3 Delete the cat

Click on the bin to delete the cat.

Sprite1

4 Add a sprite

Add the main player sprite.

Click **Choose a Sprite**.

5 Find a robot

Scroll through the sprites and click on the **Retro Robot** sprite.

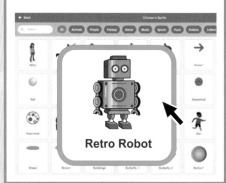

Retro Robot

6 Add the code from the Backpack

Drag each of the seven code sections from the Backpack up into the main code area.

This will add all the code from Function Freddie into your new game.

Backpack

7 Tidy up!

The code blocks will probably be piled up in a mess.

Right-click in a gap between the blocks and choose **Clean up Blocks**.

Undo
Redo
Clean up Blocks
Add Comment
Delete 61 Blocks

Your code will now be lined up neatly!

8 Prepare the background

Stage
Backdrops

Click the **Stage** icon.

Backdrops

Click the **Backdrops** tab.

Convert to Bitmap

Click the **Convert to Bitmap** button.

9 Draw the first level

Use the drawing tools to draw a circuit board for the robot to travel around.

Use the different shape tools to make your background. Look back through the book for help.

You can draw quite a simple background to start with and add more details later.

Make sure you draw a different colour on top of the microchip platforms, and use a lighter grey for the background wires.

10 Adapt your code

Go through your code now and make some changes so that the game works properly:

- In the **define getThingsReady** block, change the size from 15% to around 30%.
- In the **define moveUpOrDown** block, change the colour you are sensing from dark green to the grey colour on top of the microchips.
- In the **define checkHitWallThenMove** block, change the colour from the brown walls to the black colour of the big microchips.
- In the **define checkEndOfLevel** block, make sure the orange colour is changed to the exact shade of the door you have drawn.

 Test your code. If you have problems, check you added all seven code sections from the Backpack and that the colours are all set correctly. Then, design some more levels for your game!

Game Mods

After you have coded a game and tried the challenges, there are still lots of extra things you can add to make your game even better! In this section there are some exciting ways to modify your platform games. Experiment and have fun with your code.

Before you start using this section, load a game you have finished coding. Then, choose one of the mods to use.

> Mods are ways to change a game. Mods is short for modifications.

A: Moving Clouds

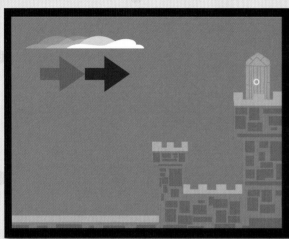

Lots of games have objects in the background. You can always draw trees onto your backdrops or add other sprites. But why not make these objects move? Moving clouds won't change how your game plays but will make it look much more professional – like a real game!

A1 Add a sprite

Click **Choose a Sprite**.

A2 Find a cloud

Scroll through the sprites and click on the **Clouds** sprite.

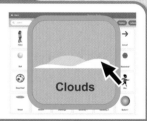

Clouds

A3 Code the cloud

Select the **Code** tab and add these code blocks:

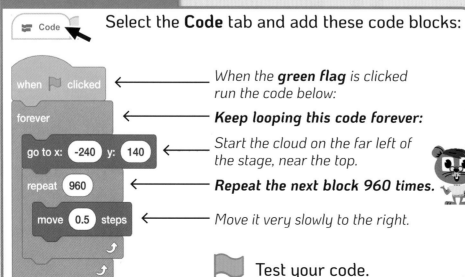

when 🏳 clicked ← *When the **green flag** is clicked run the code below:*

forever ← ***Keep looping this code forever:***

go to x: -240 y: 140 ← *Start the cloud on the far left of the stage, near the top.*

repeat 960 ← ***Repeat the next block 960 times.***

move 0.5 steps ← *Move it very slowly to the right.*

🏳 Test your code.

> The stage is 480 steps wide. So, we need to repeat moving half a step, 960 times.

> Duplicate the finished cloud to make another one. Try out different go to x and y values.